200 darkroom tips – Colour

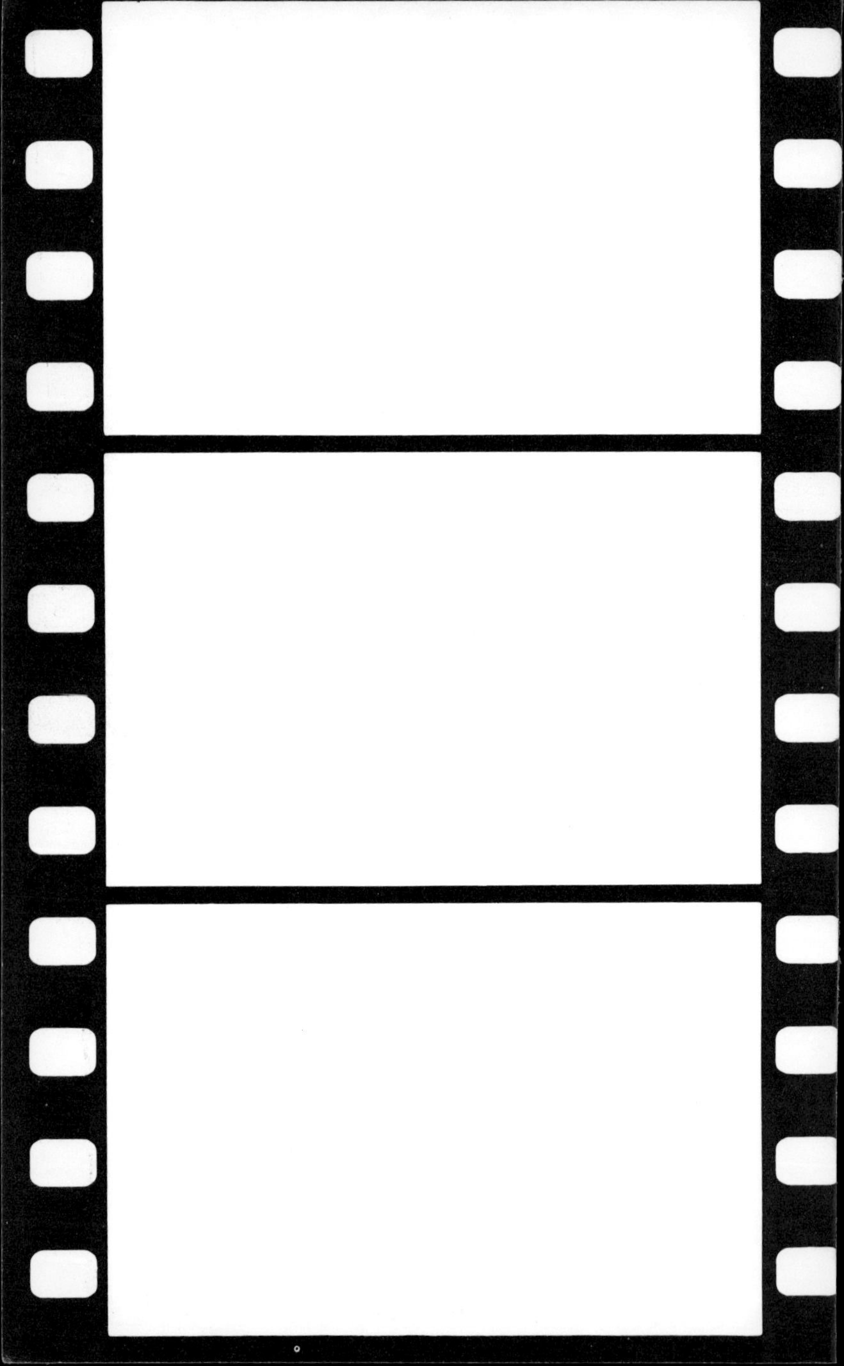

COLOUR

200 darkroom tips

By
Jan van Welzen

Translated by Mike Shields
for Cave Translations Ltd, London

Edited by R. H. Mason F.I.I.P. Hon F.R.P.S.

FOUNTAIN PRESS
Argus Books, Watford, Herts, England

ISBN 0 85242 574 0

Argus Books Ltd,
14 St James Rd,
Watford
Herts,
England

Printed Offset Litho in Great Britain by
Pindar Print, Scarborough

Contents

Introduction

When I accepted the commission to write a set of 200 darkroom tips for colour work, I had to ask myself quite seriously whether it was possible to produce 200 useful tips – taking the word "tip" in its most literal sense.

Looked at that way, the task is impossible. What you inevitably end up with is a collection of instructions, notes, personal preferences and experiences, and one or two novelties. The object, therefore, had simply to be the collection of as large a number as possible of practical tips aimed at improving your colour work. And, although they should be handy, there should also be a few designed to bring your work up to a new and higher level of achievement.

Colour work is on the increase. And, since there are so many different systems on the market to confuse the amateur, I have tried to bear him in mind when compiling these tips. This book is thus designed for people who want to do *everything* themselves. If you find that it has in any way improved your standard of work, I shall have achieved my objective.

Just a final note – the book is not entirely random. The tips are collected under headings so that you can look up what you need to know to overcome any particular problem.

1. General

Although it is possible to work in colour without a particularly deep knowledge of colour theory, I think I ought to give one or two tips on the subject. However, in many cases they are more like personal opinions, gained through my own experience.

1 **It's not difficult**

The days when do-it-yourself colour processing was a thing of great difficulty are long gone. If anybody tries to tell you that it is difficult, don't believe him! All you need is a small amount of theory, a little skill, and some essential equipment that should be as high-quality as you can afford.

This is true no matter what hobby you want to take up – photography, fishing or whatever. Which is probably why you are seeking advice anyway. This little book of tips, along with other publications, is one way of getting the information you need. Another good source of help and advice is a responsible photographic dealer. He will be able to guide you through the maze of products that have come on to the market in recent years which ensure that – once you find out which ones you want to use – do-it-yourself colour processing is not really difficult at all.

2 **Don't worry about colour theory**

Many amateurs who would like to do their own processing are put off by the apparent need to absorb a great amount of theory. They shouldn't be. While a certain amount of knowledge is naturally very useful, you won't have to pass any exams or burn any midnight oil slogging through textbooks on colour theory.

It will be necessary for you to know a little about the additive and subtractive methods, of course, and familiarity with the complementary colours will be helpful. But you certainly don't need to understand the chemical details of what happens to the film in the various baths that are used in colour processing. Lack of a theoretical knowledge of these things, therefore, is no impediment to the practical worker, apart from the odd couple of details such as those mentioned above.

3

The colour circle

One useful method of sorting yourself out on complementary colours is a print of a so-called "colours circle". You can make one for yourself by copying the small-scale reproduction given in this book. Its use is very simple; to find the complement of a given colour, just take a line from it, through the centre and to the opposite side of the circle. For example, in the subtractive method (see tip 6), too much use of the yellow filter will result in a reduction in the blue content of the picture. When we talk about filter methods, you will find this circle of colours very useful.

4

Easier than black-and-white?

In some ways, yes, believe it or not. I would say without hesitation that, if you have never done any processing before, start with colour rather than black-and-white.

One of the main arguments in favour of this point of view is that you can easily see if a photo has a dominant colour – that is, if it is being adversely affected because of an overall cast of a particular colour. In black-and-white work, the choice of the right grade of paper is something that many people still haven't mastered after years of work. This is because we see the world in terms of colour and not of grey, black and white. Once you get into the way of filtering out a colour cast by using the right methods and equipment, colour processing is very simple. There are those who won't agree with this argument, but I think it has a lot to commend it.

5

Additive colour mixing

You probably know already that light is made up of a mixture of colours, and that mixtures of given colours produce further, predictable colours. If we take three light sources in the three primary colours – red, blue and green – and project them all onto one spot, the result will be white. If we take one colour away, we get the complementary colours of yellow, purple, or blue-green respectively. These complementary colours are shown in the colour circle which we talked about in tip 3.

If we work with three filters in these primary colours, and use them to make three separate exposures – usually with different times – then we can produce a colour positive from a colour negative. And that, in a few words, is the additive process.

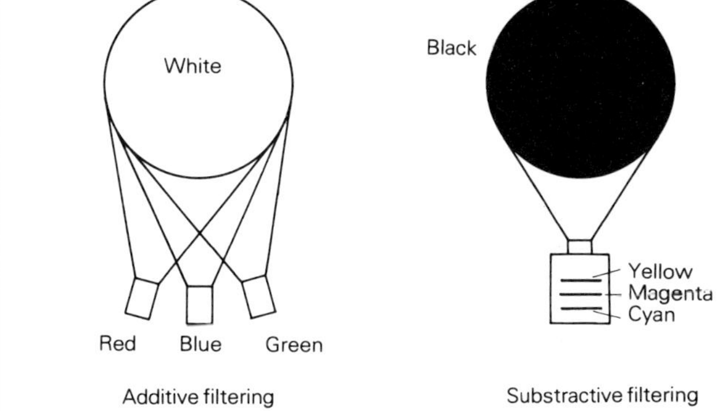

6 **Subtractive colour mixing**

This is the opposite of the additive process, and makes use of three filters, coloured yellow, magenta, and cyan. Whereas, with the additive method, we used the filters to add light to the image, here we superimpose them so as to take it away.

Since each filter absorbs one third of the spectrum, the result of putting three such filters together would be black. However, if filters of lower intensity are used, various densities of grey will be produced. This is because the three spectral regions are being absorbed evenly.

Both systems are in use, but the subtractive method is now the most popular with both amateurs and professionals. There are advantages and disadvantages in both methods, but, on balance, the subtractive is easier and more reliable.

7 **So which one . . . . . additive?**

Personally, I reckon that this method requires more mental effort. You've really got to be on your toes, so to speak, the whole time. If the test comes out too yellow, you've got to increase the blue filtering, and I have always found the business of working out the exposure for each filter very time consuming. It is also rather more difficult to get rid of a particular colour cast. Moreover, because you have to make three separate exposures, there is more likelihood of the print or the negative carrier moving between exposures, thus blurring the final picture. Other disadvantages of this method are that you cannot use the well-known "dodging" techniques of holding-back or burning-in, nor can you alter the exposure of any given part of the picture in order to improve the overall effect. To be absolutely accurate, you can, but it would have to be repeated exactly in each of three different exposures, which would be far from easy to get right. There is little to be said for this method from the point of view of the amateur except that the filter packs are cheaper.

8

. . . . . or additive?

The critical attitude of the previous tip shouldn't be taken as a complete condemnation of the additive method. It is possible to get good results by this method and, some colour processing centres use it. However, they've got electronically controlled equipment to help them. There is a system suitable for the amateur, and we will talk about that in tip 113.

It is also possible, of course, to get good results yourself by trial and error methods. As your knowledge of colour theory improves you may find the additive method useful.

9

. . . . or subtractive?

As I've already made clear in the previous two tips, I reckon that this method is unbeatable for the amateur. All you need is a set of subtractive filters (see tips 97-99) and a diffuser to go over the lens. The set will consist of filters in the complementary colours of yellow, magenta and cyan. The big advantage with this method is that, if there is a colour cast, you take that colour out of the filter pack. Yellow for a yellow cast, yellow and cyan for a green cast and yellow and magenta for a red cast, and so on. This is where the colour circle comes in handy. Again, only one exposure is needed, so that exposure tricks such as burning-in and holding-back are possible. This really is the best system for the beginner to use, even if the filter kits are a bit more expensive.

10

Colour temperature

You probably think of daylight and the light that comes from the usual type of light bulb as being more or less "white", but this in fact is quite erroneous. Light comes in many different forms, and much light that is apparently white is in fact coloured.

This is measured by means of "colour temperature" expressed in degrees Kelvin. Precisely what this means we won't go into here – it is far too advanced for a book like this, and you don't need to know anyway.

What you *do* need to know is that films are designed for a given value of colour temperature. For artificial light, the temperature is about 3100K, while for noon daylight under cloud it is about 5600K. If you take a photo in the evening you will find that, because the light is redder than it is at midday (ie it has a lower colour temperature), the picture will tend to have a red or orange cast which may have to be removed during processing.

11

Reflections

Sometimes, light reflected from a coloured surface affects the colour of other things nearby. In most cases we don't notice this but the eye of the camera, unlike our own, sees only what is there. If, for example, your subject has been placed near an orange-coloured surface, it will be suffused with an orange glow. Moreover, this effect cannot be removed by filters because, in doing so, a filter would also affect the other colours in the photograph. It is far better to take more care at the time of the photograph.
The same sort of thing can happen in your darkroom, if you're not careful. A strongly-coloured surface can reflect light from the enlarger on to the surface of the paper and adversely affect the colour of your print. From my own experience, I would advise you not to go in for brightly-coloured developing tanks – a neutral grey is better for the colour darkroom, as indeed is white or black.

12

Colour negative/paper/chemical combinations

At one time it was good advice to use Kodak chemicals with Kodak papers and Agfa chemicals with Agfa papers. This no longer applies because a number of chemical manufacturers, notably May & Baker, Patersons, Photo Technology and Tetenal have produced kits which are fully compatible and which are efficient and reliable. Photo Technology have produced a kit called Photocolor 11 which will process both colour negatives and colour papers such as Kodak's 74 RC and it has had a world wide success, not only because of its efficiency but because it costs about $^1/_3$rd less than Kodak C41 (for negatives) and Ektaprint 3 (for papers). They also produce Photochrome R which is for processing Kodak 14 RC reversal paper to make prints direct from transparencies. It is a lot cheaper than Ektachrome E3 chemicals.

13

Masked and unmasked films

Putting it as simply as possible, the mask in a colour film is a yellow-orange layer that separates the various colour layers of which the film is made up. In the past, these layers caused a certain amount of distortion as light passed from one to the other. Nowadays, all makes of negative colour films have built in orange masking but Kodacolor and Vericolor have lighter masking than most.

2. The darkroom for colour processing

Obviously, in a section like this, there are a lot of tips that you could easily find elsewhere. For this reason, I have tried to keep to tips that deal particularly with the problems of a *colour* darkroom.

14

The colour darkroom

Basically, the colour darkroom doesn't differ from the black-and-white darkroom but the colour darkroom must be altogether more efficient. A lot of processes take up more time, and you will need to do a lot more checking before you can start printing; which means that you must be prepared to spend more time in the dark. So, if you haven't anywhere to sit, there's a danger that, in leaning against a bench, you'll knock something down, because the light in a colour darkroom is less than usual, too.

So the first piece of advice I will give you is this: get rid of anything you don't need for colour processing. It only takes up valuable work room and gets in your way.

15

Layout

The best layout of working surfaces, etc, will vary with what is available and with personal preference, but I myself go for the so-called "L-shaped room", with one leg for wet working and the other for dry. On the wet side go the developing dishes, heaters, bottles and so on, and on the dry side sits the enlarger, along with negs, paper and other accessories. A swivel stool is also a great help.

You could, alternatively, have one bench on each wall (as shown in the lower diagram opposite), with you sitting in between them.

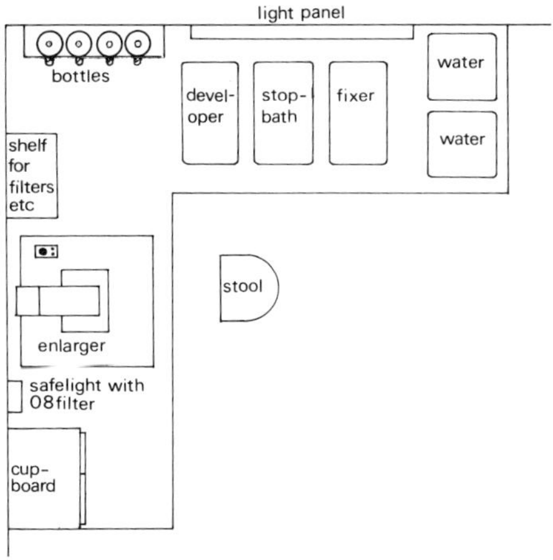

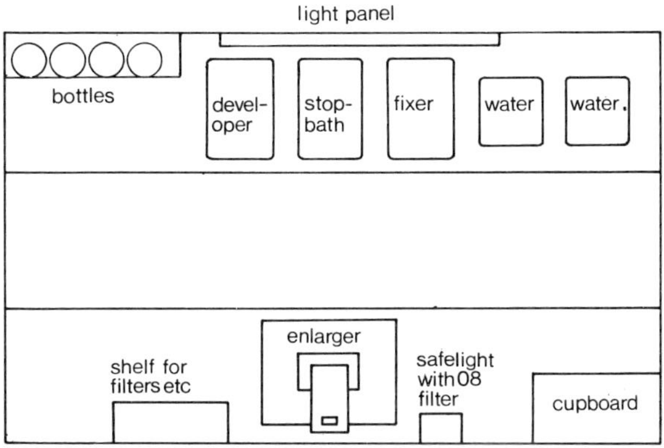

Illumination

This is often a cause of worry to beginners, who tend to think that you can't have any light at all in a darkroom intended for colour work. Of course, this isn't true: we can have a very deep brownish-green coloured safelight. With this type of filter and a 15-watt lamp, the amount of light is minimal and the distance from the light to any exposed material should not be less than 70cm. (5 ft)

On no account be tempted to try a larger bulb in your safelight. In the first place it will probably melt your filter but, even if it doesn't, the light output will almost certainly be too great for your materials. On the whole it is better to try and work in complete darkness which is essential in any case for developing colour films.

17

Lighting equipment

Those amateurs who cannot work in the dark tend to go for safelights of 9 × 12 cm format. However, a lamp with a greater area will give more light, despite the fact that it still uses the same 15-watt bulb.

Durst market two rather nice darkroom lights under the names of Safil and Sanat. The Safil has five different colour filters. The Sanat, however, uses a 15-volt, 15-watt sodium vapour lamp as its light source. The theory behind this is that there is a "gap" in the colour sensitivity of papers between red and yellow, and the light from this type of lamp is right in that gap. Because of this, it can give out a little more light without risk of damage to the photo-sensitive papers if kept at a distance. It also means that you can find pieces of film before you've walked over them a couple of times!

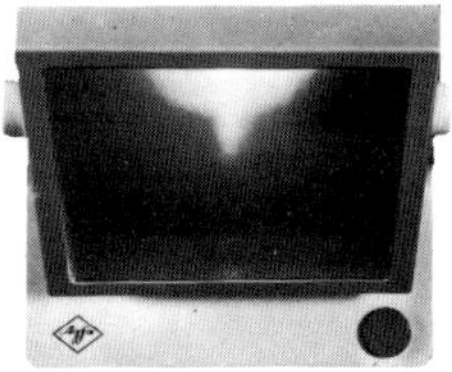

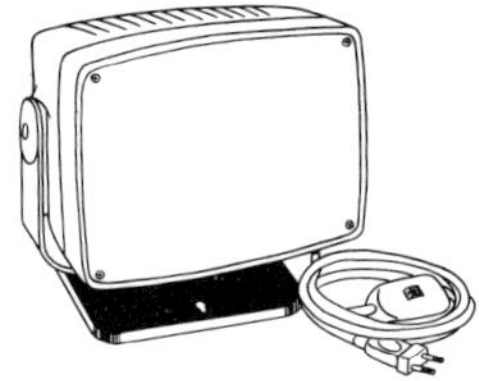

Left: A typical darkroom lamp.

Right: The Durst Sanat.

Opposite: It's a good idea to make a couple of shelves to go at either side of your enlarger.

18

Give your eyes a chance

In both the previous tips, I have referred to the very restricted brown filter for your safelight. Note that I still make regular use of my ordinary yellow-green safelight as well but not, of course, for processing.

What I do is to switch this on when I first put out the main lighting, and use this for the first ten minutes or so, until my eyes get used to the different colour and level of lighting. During this time I get things out and generally prepare to work. Then, when I'm fully accustomed to the part-darkness, I put out the yellow-green light and switch the brown light on.

At the end of the process, when the prints are in the fixing bath, you can reverse this acclimatization procedure. Put on the yellow-green safelight for a few minutes before eventually switching on the main lighting. I find this a useful and quite safe way of moving back to normal lighting levels. If you work with a developing tank, then of course it won't be necessary to wait until the end before coming back to normal lighting.

19

Handy shelves

There are always things you need to have to hand in a darkroom – things like a pencil and notepaper, scissors (constantly!), and an anti-static cloth. If you have room, there are of course many other things you could name, too: a set of filters, timer, spare lamp, spare lens and so on.

Because of the low lighting level, you should try to have these things in a given place, so that you can find them easily. For this reason, therefore, it is a good idea to fix up a couple of shelves on either side of your enlarger. They cost very little, and will be used more than most other things in the darkroom. In fact, you should fix up as many shelves as possible – you'll always find a use for them.

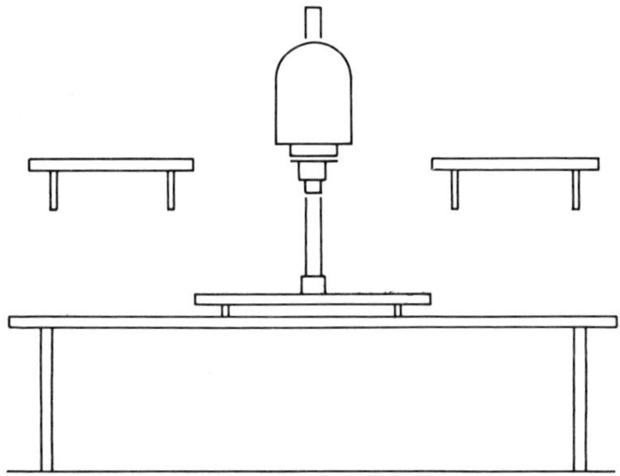

20

Making your darkroom dark

One of the important things about a good darkroom is that, despite the very limited level of lighting you can use, you should be able to see as well as possible. The walls, therefore, should be light coloured so as to make the most of what light there is.

When it comes to keeping the light out, a smallish window can best be covered with hardboard, so as to avoid the dust which curtains attract and trap. The gaps at the edges can be sealed with black rubber strip, which is available in various widths and can be stuck to the hardboard with a suitable adhesive.

For larger windows, it is best to use a blackout curtain. These are made from a special material which consists of two layers of linen with rubber in between; they are very flexible, however, and can be used over ordinary curtains. Although they are more liable to trap dust than shutters, they are still far better in this respect than ordinary curtains.

21 **Checking for unwanted light**

Even a small amount of light is dangerous in a darkroom, since it can lead to fogging and colour casts on your photographs. You should always remember that your enlarger is likely to be the culprit in this respect. Some enlargers – and not necessarily old ones – leak from the lamphouse or negative carrier, and this can seriously affect the quality of your finished work.

If you want to check the light-tightness of your darkroom, leave a piece of photographic paper partly covered (with a coin, say) somewhere in the darkroom for about five minutes with the enlarger switched on. Then develop the paper. If it comes out a normal white, then everything is all right but if there is any evidence that the uncovered part has been exposed to light you've got a leak and will have to do something about it.

22 **Heating**

Apart from the fact that working in a freezing cold darkroom in the depths of winter is not very funny, heating is needed in order to keep the working temperature of the processes at the right level.

Even if you have dish heaters, the upper surface of the solutions will rapidly lose heat to cold air unless you prevent this. How much heat you lose depends, of course, on the size of the dish, but you will certainly lose some.

In view of what we have said about light-tightness, you should never choose any kind of heater with a radiant element or a visible flame, such as a paraffin heater or an electric fire. Best of all is a central-heating radiator, if one can be made available.

23 **Dust**

If anything, it is even more important to keep dust away from colour work than from black-and-white. The white marks left by dust when it is allowed to collect on glasses and negatives are very unsightly on a colour print. While it is possible – if tedious – to touch up a black-and-white print that is dust-marked, it is almost out of the question to do it against backgrounds which vary through all the colours of the spectrum. In this case, prevention is very much better than cure.

Rules for avoiding dust are quite simple. If there are windows, don't use curtains (see also tip 20). A smooth floor free of rugs or carpets is best. Dust-brushes and anti-static cloths, too, are not luxuries. Also, don't move around in the darkroom any more than you have to – it stirs up the dust.

24

Hot water

If you decide to go in for a warm working environment, one factor you might overlook is the washing water. You should not lose sight of the fact that, in these rather more critical processes, colour casts can also be caused by incorrect washing temperatures. The most attractive solution, of course, is to have hot and cold running water in your darkroom, or at least to have a tube leading to a boiler or geyser.

However, if you don't happen to have access to such luxurious quarters, there is a little gadget available that fixes to the wall and heats water electrically. It is very simple in operation, and just connects to the cold tap with a hose.

Of course, you can always make a thermostatically-controlled washing tank yourself if you have the room for it, or buy one of the several makes now available such as the Jobo, Paterson or Wilkinson.

25

Running water

This is something you should have if at all possible, because there are any number of processes in which running water is almost essential. Many of the faults that can occur in prints can be prevented at a stroke, as it were, by the provision of running water.

If running water is out of the question, then you should try to provide yourself with a couple of pretty big plastic tanks. This is a good solution where the darkroom is not too far from the tap.

Whatever you do, don't economize on washing water. If you can't arrange running water, make sure that you change the water in the tanks often so as to prevent contamination.

26

Careful with chemicals

Although you shouldn't dispose of chemicals down a domestic sink at all, I would advise that, if you ever have to, you should take great care to wash out the sink well and truly with a lot of running water afterwards.

More than with black and white, you must take care to wash out dishes and tanks, because the least trace of chemicals can ruin hours of careful work. And you should keep all sensitive materials in a cool place, preferably in a refrigerator.

Perhaps you think that it is superfluous to advise you to keep your darkroom tidy. Of course, if the room is used for other purposes, then you'll have to clear everything away after you, although you will be able to leave some things out if it is used solely as a darkroom. But in either case, you will find that tidiness pays – "a place for everything and everything in its place" is a phrase that could have been coined for darkrooms!

3. Negatives

It is very important and quite easy to develop your own films, especially with the materials we have available for this task today. To help people who want to do it themselves, I have devoted a member of tips to the subject.

27

Developing films yourself . . . .
What, me? I can almost hear you saying – can't possibly develop my own colour films – takes too much time and far too complicated. Prints can be repeated but if a film's spoilt it's gone forever, so it's safer to send it a dealer or a chemist.
Well, before you convince yourself of all that consider that in spite of all the care that processing houses give to films they occasionally slip up. Some houses are worse than others and they sometimes scratch films, tear them or even lose them. The trouble is that when you take your films to a photo dealer or a chemist you don't know which type of processing house he deals with.
There are also a number of big firms to whom you can mail your films direct. Here again, you have no means of knowing which are reliable and which are not.
Apart from all that, colour film processing has been simplified and there is no thrill like that of seeing your film come out in your own darkroom in full colour, and without having to wait a week or more for it.

28

. . . . yes, you!
It's not going to cost you much to develop films. In fact, if you already have a developing tank, you can use it for colour films just as well as for black-and-white. What you can do, if you wish, is to get a couple of extra spirals and keep these separate for colour work if you think you'll still be doing black-and-white work as well. You can get spare spirals for most makes of tank.
What type of tank should you use? Several manufacturers, including Durst, Jobo and Paterson produce tanks with self loading spirals. The stainless steel tanks are very nice to use and will certainly last, but they are also more expensive than plastic. There are also very good 'daylight tanks,' the Jobo 2400 and the Agfa Rondinax into which a film can be loaded in normal lighting. It is even possible to develop part of a film with these tanks and that can be very useful on occasions.

29

If a thing's worth doing . . . .

. . . . it's worth doing well! So, now that you know that developing your own colour films isn't going to be impossibly difficult, perhaps we can find out just what is entailed. And here I am going to suggest that you keep precisely to the working methods given in these tips.

One of the things it's absolutely essential to keep under control if excessive grain and several other nasty faults are to be avoided is the temperature of the process. So you will need a good, easy-to-read thermometer. Don't forget, either, that washing between processes must be accurately temperature-controlled. Drying also has to be done with the greatest care for it is here that some of the worst faults can occur.

30

Should you experiment with developers?

Not at first. Later, perhaps, you may experiment but for the moment keep to what you know. I am no advocate of making up your own developers for colour work; the risks are too great. It's one thing to mess about with developers for prints – they are replaceable, but films aren't so perhaps it's better not to experiment.

This is as good a time as any to issue a warning about mixing developers in powder form. For a start, the inhalation of these powders is not good for anyone's health and, for another, they are easily spread about so that they contaminate other materials thereby causing a lot of trouble. The trend nowadays is towards ready-made solutions and this is a step in the right direction.

31

Films

If you want to use Kodak, then I can recommend Kodacolor II film (80 ASA/20 DIN). This is a high quality film which has very light masking, (see tip 13), gives a fine grain result and clean crisp colour reproduction.

Vericolor II is designed for the professional, but has the same outstanding characteristics as Kodacolor II film. The colour balance is somewhat more critical. It is intended for commercial photography and it will not keep so well as Kodacolor. It is an ideal film for portrait work.

Agfa-Gevaert market CNS-II film and Agfacolor 80 S. The CNS-II is a considerable improvement on the old CNS films. It is quite a lot lighter, has better grain properties and gives somewhat warmer colours than Kodak films. Agfacolor 80 S is the professional version of this film and it has a wider exposure latitude than Kodak Vericolor II. Both Agfa films have the normal orange masks and a speed of 80 ASA (20 Din). Agfa, Fuji, Kodak and Sakura also make colour negative films with a speed of 400 ASA (27 DIN)

32

Chemicals for colour developers

There are at present quite a number of do-it-yourself colour negative developing kits on the market.

Apart from those marketed by the mighty Kodak there are several other developing kits produced by well-known chemical firms. With most of them, developing colour film is no more difficult than developing black-and-white. There is always the sub-standard bargain of course but, if you use the right stuff and work accurately you should have no problems.

33

Developing Kodacolor II

There is a special one-pint (473 ml) kit available for do-it-yourself developing of Kodacolor II films; this is the Kodak C-41 kit.

With this kit, it is possible to develop a film in less than 30 minutes. The kit comprises four solutions – developer, bleach, fixer and stabilizer. The developer, fixer and stabilizer are provided in the form of concentrated solutions, while the bleach is made up from three components, two of which are solutions and one a powder.

The developer solution is provided in double quantity because the other solutions have twice the capacity of the developer. When made up the developer will keep for four weeks and the other solutions for eight.

The capacity is equivalent to six 36-shot miniature-format films. Used with Vericolor II in small-capacity tanks, however, this kit will only process four 35 mm films of 36 shots.

The Kodak C41 process

Solution	Temperature	Time (mins)*	Total time
Developer	37.8°C (±.15°C)	$3\frac{1}{4}$	$3\frac{1}{4}$
Bleach	24-41°C	$4\frac{1}{2}$	$7\frac{3}{4}$
From this point on the process can be carried out in normal room lighting if desired.			
Washing	38°C (± 3°C)	1	$8\frac{3}{4}$
Fixer	24-41°C	$4\frac{1}{2}$	$13\frac{1}{4}$
Washing	38°C (± 3°C)	$3\frac{1}{2}$	$16\frac{3}{4}$
Stabilizer	24-41°C	$1\frac{1}{4}$	18
Drying	24-41°C	10-20	28-38

*including 10 seconds for pouring out. Temperature is highly critical.

34

The Agfacolor N satz kit

I can certainly recommend this kit for all Agfacolor negative films. It comprises five solutions:

a. Colour developer
b. Intermediate bath
c. Bleach
d. Fixer
c. Stabilizer

You can develop six 36-shot 35mm films with a one-litre kit. Total working time including washing is 52 minutes. This makes it quite a lengthy process, but it is simple and certainly not expensive. The solutions keep well, too – developer for about six weeks, and other solutions about three months. Other details can be learned from the instruction leaflet.

35

Colour negative developing kits

The principal kits available in the U.K. for processing colour negatives are Agfacolor, Kodak C41, Paterson Acucolor 2 and Photocolor II. These will process all Type II colour films which are compatible with C41 chemistry except Agfacolor which is for Agfa films. Type II films include Kodacolor II, Kodacolor 400, Vericolor II, Fujicolor II, Fujicolor 400, Sakuracolor II, Sakuracolor 400 and Boots Colourprint II.

Tetenal make a kit called N1 which is a four bath process for Agfacolor. All the others are four bath processes except Photocolor II which is only three and as a result is easily the quickest. It takes only 12½ minutes including pre-heating and washing. The operating temperature is 38°C(100°F) for the colour developer although it can be reduced to 96°F by lengthening the development time. The concentrates keep for about 1 year unopened and working strength developer will keep for about 6 weeks in an airtight bottle. Squeezing the bottles used for concentrates can serve this purpose. Bleach-fix will keep for at least 8 weeks in half-filled bottles because its action is actually improved by aeration. A one litre kit of Photocolor II will process at least five 35 mm 36 exposure films or five 120 roll films but a great advantage is that if you only process, say, one film the rest can be used for paper processing.

Negative processing with Photocolor II

If a tank for developing black and white films is available the only extra item you are likely to need is an accurate thermometer reading up to 40°C (105°F). The kit consists of liquid concentrates – Colour developer, Bleach-Fix and an Additive which is only used for adding to the colour developer when using it for colour paper processing. The stop bath you provide yourself and it can be 1% acetic acid or 1% of Indicol. No stabiliser is required.

The tank should be loaded in total darkness in the usual way and the solutions diluted 1+2 for the colour developer and 1+1 for the bleach-fix warmed up to 38°C (100°F). It will also be necessary to heat a quantity of water (about $\frac{1}{2}$ tankful) up to 40°C (105°F) for pre-heating.

The processing sequence is:-

Pre-heat tank with water at 40°C (105°F)	1 minute
Colour development at 38°C (100°F)	$2\frac{3}{4}$ minutes
Stop Bath at 35°C-40°C (95°-104°F)	$\frac{1}{2}$ minute
Bleach-fixing at 35°C-40°C (95°-104°F)	3 minutes
Washing with running water or frequent changes at 30°C-35°(86°-95°F)	5 minutes
Total Time . . .	$12\frac{1}{4}$ minutes

Washing can be done at lower temperatures if times are extended accordingly.

Typical processing times with 4 bath chemicals.

Agfacolour CNS-2	20°C	14 min.	4 min.	12 min.	7 min.	20 min.	10 min.
Agfacolour 80-S	20°C	14 min.	4 min.	12 min.	7 min.	20 min.	10 min.
Orwocolour NC-19Mask	20°C	11 min.	4 min.	12 min.	7 min.	20 min.	10 min.
Kodacolor II	20°C	11 min.	4 min.	12 min.	7 min.	10 min.	10 min.
Vericolor II	21°C	11 min.	4 min.	12 min.	7 min.	10 min.	10 min.
Fujicolor F-II	20°C	7 min.	4 min.	12 min.	7 min.	10 min.	10 min.
3M color print	20°C	9 min.	4 min.	12 min.	7 min.	10 min.	10 min.
Turacolor II	20°C	7 min.	4 min.	12 min.	7 min.	10 min.	10 min.

37 **Paterson Acucolor 2**

Acucolor 2, like Photocolor II, is a British made kit for processing colour negative films and it comes in four liquid concentrates to make 1 litre of each solution. These quantities are sufficient to process twelve Type 2 35 mm or 120 roll films. Smaller quantities can be mixed if desired and the storage life of the colour developer concentrate unopened is about six months, and about six weeks after dilution if stored in brown glass bottles, free from air space. Alternatively use the concertina bottles mentioned in Tip 79.
The stop bath provided is Paterson Acustop but you could equally well use 1% acetic acid or 1% Indicol. It's sole purpose is to stop development quickly and this makes for precise timing.

The sequence of processing steps is:-

Colour development at 37.8°C (100°F)	3¼ minutes
Stop Bath at 38°C (100°F)	½ minute
Rinse with water at 38°C (100°F)	½ minute
Bleach-Fix at 38°C (100°°F)	6½ minutes
Wash in running water at 25°-38°C (75°-100°F)	3¼ minutes
Stabilize at 25°-38°C (75°-100°F)	1½ minutes
Total Time . . .	15 minutes

The tolerance for the temperature of the colour developer is only ± 0.15°C (+¼°F) and developing at other temperatures with extended times is not recommended.

38 **Developing tanks.**

As I've already mentioned you can use your normal black and white film developing tanks for colour as well but it is very important that they are kept chemically clean to avoid contamination from one film to the next. Plastic tanks like the Durst and the popular Paterson System 4 should be kept in a warm place as plastic does not take up heat so easily as metal. The Paterson tank has the advantage of being extremely quick to fill and empty thus making precise timing possible. Stainless steel tanks are easy to keep clean and quick to heat but rather slow to fill and very expensive. Regular agitation whether by rotating the spiral or upturning the tank is most important and the instructions given with the kits should be closely followed. Of course, if you are the lucky owner of a mechanised processor like the Jobo, agitation is no problem but you must beware of too even agitation in one direction or 'waves' may be set up giving rise to uneven development streaks.

39

Keeping the temperature constant

The temperature required for all colour negative films is higher than for black and white films.
Because you must maintain these temperatures very precisely there can be some difficulty when you are changing solutions. The tank starts off at a low temperature and can – particularly in cool weather – be cooled too much. The answer is to have a bucket or a deep tank handy filled with water at just the right temperature and hold the developing tank in it. You can maintain the temperature of the water in the big tank with a tank-warmer or an aquarium heater. In this respect, as always, pay strict attention to the instructions. It also helps to keep the darkroom ambient temperature as high as possible.

40

Washing

The final washing of films differs from system to system so here is another case where instructions have to be followed.
Just letting water run into the filler hole of your tank is not good enough. A better method is to fill the tank with water and then empty it before filling it again, repeating the process several times. If the system calls for, say, 14 minutes washing, this can be something of a bother. Best of all are washing systems such as the Paterson hose or the Jobo Cascade.
After washing, the film should be treated with a wetting agent such as Johnsons 326 and allowed to drip-dry in a dust-free atmosphere. Most films need to be dry before they can be checked; Kodak films, in fact, have a blue cast when wet which disappears as the film dries.

41

Drying – its problems and solutions

While it is wet, the film is particularly susceptible to scratching and other mechanical damage and so you should aim to get it dry as quickly and as safely as possible. After the final wash, the film can be treated with a proprietary hardener, or you can add 15 ml of 37% formalin per litre to the wash water.
If the film does get scratched there is a Tetenal product called Repolisan which is added to the final wash water. I've cured some bad scratches with this. After washing with Repolisan you let the film drip dry and, if the scratches aren't too deep, they just disappear as the film dries.

4. Equipment

There is so much around in the line of equipment nowadays that the amateur might be justified in feeling a little dazed by it all. This section is intended to help you out of that daze by naming the most important items.

42

The enlarger for colour
The most important single piece of equipment is, of course, your enlarger, and so it must achieve a certain standard of quality. The factors that affect the quality of the enlarger are the optical system, the illumination system, the ease of operation, and the potential usefulness. What I mean by potential usefulness will be explained more fully in the following tip. Ease of operation is a more important factor than you might suppose, too, especially since the enlarger has to be operated in the dark or by the sparse light of a darkroom safelight.
And as to optics, you should remember that the condensers are most important, and should provide even light all over the baseboard. The lens itself must, of course, be colour-corrected and as good as the one on the camera.

43

Miniature format or 6 × 6 cm?
If you are buying or renewing your enlarger, this is a question to which you'll have to give a little thought. You may well think "I have a miniature camera, so all I'll need will be a 35 mm enlarger". Or if you have a 6 × 6 cm camera, you might think the reverse. But, surely, it will be best of all to get an enlarger that handles both formats? They can be obtained, in the form of 6 × 6 cm enlargers with facilities for 35 mm or less. Later in your exploration of the techniques of colour photography, you may find that you want to make intermediate negatives, and the usual format for these is 6 × 6 cm. You can therefore seriously limit yourself by settling for just a miniature format enlarger, so think awhile before you make your final decision. There is more information on experimental techniques in Section 10.

44

Should you have a filter drawer?

First of all, what is it? A filter drawer is a holder placed between the bulb and the lens in which one or more filters can be inserted, so as to remove any colour cast there might be in the negative. If your enlarger is so equipped, then you can straight away use the subtractive method of printing. (see tip 9)

If you happen to have an older type of enlarger without a built-in filter drawer this naturally does not preclude you from working in colour. In this case you can use the additive method in which the filters are located underneath the enlarger lens (see tip 8).

There are also enlargers, for example the Durst 601 or Durst 605, for which a special colour head can be bought or which have one built in. In my own opinion these filter heads make colour printing much easier (see tip 173).

45

Reducing the size of the filter drawer

Some enlargers, such as the Durst M-601, have a filter drawer which is larger than the current standard filter size of 7 × 7 cm. Despite the fact that many users of this type of enlarger will be working with colour heads, there are occasions when you want to use an extra filter to sort out a special problem. What I do with my own Durst is to make up a little frame of stiff black card to use as a mask. On the edges of this I stick thin strips of wood to hold the whole thing squarely and stiffen it up. You can do this for most enlargers, and it doesn't affect the filter.

46

Light distribution

The optical system of an enlarger consists of a lamp, and several lenses, at least one of which is a condenser lens. The function of this lens is to distribute the light from the lamp so that the negative is evenly illuminated.

Uneven illumination is undesirable in black-and-white photography but in colour work it is absolutely fatal.

Put more accurately, it is theoretically possible to do some slight correction for uneven illumination if you are using the subtractive method but there's nothing you can do about it if you use the additive method.

In either case, therefore, you should check your enlarger very carefully. Make a test exposure at the widest aperture of your lens by placing a piece of paper on the baseboard without a negative in the carrier. After about 4 minutes exposure you should carefully examine the result. If there is any darkening at the corners of the print you will have to centre or adjust the lamp.

47

Lamp wattage

You can sometimes improve the light distribution of your enlarger by using a 150-watt bulb in place of the standard 75-watt. This has its effect because of the physically larger bulb. Naturally, the new bulb must fit the enlarger, and you must also be sure that your ventilation system can cope with the greater heat output. If you can use it, the greater light output can also be useful when you have denser negatives to print from, especially if you want to make large prints.

The colour of the light from an ordinary enlarger bulb is not the same as that from the 12v 100w halogen bulb, which is used in a colour head. This must always be borne in mind if you use an ordinary lamp with a mixing head. An extra addition of yellow and magenta filters will be needed in order to correct the light output.

48

The lamp – halogen or conventional?

A conventional bulb such as the Philips Photorescenta gives out a light that is much more yellow than a halogen bulb, and also produces less light for a given wattage. Also, after a while, the colour of the light changes so that, if you have to renew a bulb in the middle of a processing session, you'll have to adjust the filtration to allow for it. If you use a conventional bulb in combination with an analyser, it is somewhat better.

The halogen lamp, on the other hand, maintains its colour throughout its working life and thus gives no trouble in this respect. You will find, however, that it is not possible to use a halogen lamp in an old-fashioned type of enlarger and a step down transformer from 240 volts to 12 volts is essential when using halogen bulbs in modern enlarger heads.

49

The heat filter

Anyone working with loose filters in a filter drawer should invest in a heat filter. There is a heat filter available for all makes of enlargers and in some the enlarger has the heat filter built-in. Of course, the ventilation of a good enlarger should be such that heat build-up does not occur during normal working but, in the case of long exposures, it is always best to be on the safe side.

The only trouble is that the colour of the heat filter tends to give a slight cast to the photo being exposed, and this has to be compensated for. If you use a colour mixing head, there is no need for a heat filter because you don't use gelatin filters with a low-voltage halogen lamp in a colour head.

50

Can you use your camera lens?

It may be tempting to think so but the answer is only in a very few cases. Despite what you might read in other books on photography, my advice to you is not to use your camera lens in your enlarger.

All enlarger lenses, even the cheapest, are specially designed for enlarging. They give a brighter field than that of the camera lens, which is usually too soft and not designed for working so close. There are other risks, too, such as loosening of the cement which holds the lens elements together, which are just not worth taking. It would be possible to go on about this for quite some time, but it would require rather too deep an excursion into lens theory.

The Durst Comask baseboard for various fixed formats up to 18 × 24 cm.

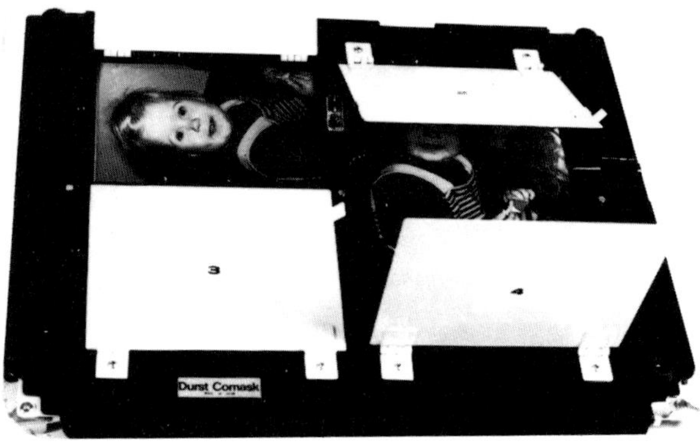

51

The baseboard

A good baseboard is just as necessary for colour work as for black-and-white, although whether you want to make borderless prints or not is up to you. This will, however, affect your choice of board. You may already have an ordinary board with adjustable masks for use in black-and-white work. Boards that allow you to make borderless prints are available from Paterson and Polysales. The Durst Comask is a special type which allows you to make prints in various formats up to 18 × 24 cm. It is very handy for making test prints because it is possible to make four 9 × 12 prints one after the other (see illustration), or you can make four test prints with different filter combinations at one setting on one sheet of 10″ × 8″ paper.

Timers

52 Since we're going to take a fairly detailed look at timers, it may be as well if we start out by making a rough classification of types. We can start with the simple alarm clocks, which are little different from those used to wake you up in the mornings, and are completely separate from the enlarger. They can be powered either by clockwork or from the mains. As they're pretty simple timers, they don't usually indicate less than half minute intervals.

Then there are switch-timers, which are normally connected between the mains and the enlarger, thereby switching it off automatically when the exposure that you set is finished. These also come in various types, the clockwork ones being the simplest and cheapest. They are also the least reliable for colour work. The electric ones are better, but best of all are the electronic ones, which ensure the highest standards of timing accuracy.

Switched timers

53 As you can see from the previous tip, I come down rather heavily in favour of electric or electronic timers. Variations in exposure time are especially important in series work in colour, and for this reason they must at all costs be avoided.

Most of these timers have an illuminated dial, and so can be seen easily in the dark (don't worry – the light from it will not affect your work). With the illuminated dial, the timer should be located not only in a handy place, but also in a place such that white light can fall on the dial thus "recharging" the luminous paint from time to time; otherwise it will lose its luminosity. This type of timer is usually calibrated in seconds. Some even go as far as tenths of seconds and have a repeat facility as well. This is very convenient if you want to make several prints from one negative.

The Durst Coltim

54 Most colour processes require you to place papers in various successive baths for differing times. Some of these time intervals, too, must be very accurately controlled. As you might imagine, the timing of a succession of processes like this can be difficult and the Durst Coltim is a boon. This handy little device has a number of tabs around the edge of its dial (rather like the tabs on a central heating control knob) which enable you to set up a number of different intervals in advance so that you don't have to reset the timer in the middle of a process. The smallest available interval is half a minute, so it is possible to set up a number of intervals such as 5 min, $1\frac{1}{2}$ min, 3 min and so on. A loud 'ping' is given at the end of each interval.

If by any chance you want to set up several successive programmes, it is possible to obtain spare dials so that you can set them up in advance and simply drop them on the timer when required. This is an extremely handy timer and I cannot recommend it too highly.

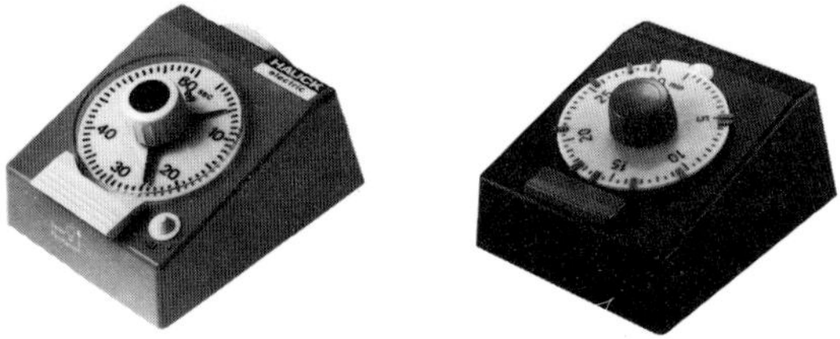

Left: The Hauck timer.

Right: The Durst Coltim.

55 Dishes

Nowadays processing in dishes is gradually being edged out by the more convenient developing drum but, if you still insist on using dishes, the first thing you should make sure of is that they are at least one size larger than the format in which you are working.
The colour of the dishes you use is not too important, but white dishes are preferable. You can always mark them with letters to identify them – D for developer, F for fixer and so on. You'll find that PVC dishes are good but beware of the inferior types that warp with heat.
If you don't have running water in your darkroom you should equip yourself with a couple of large plastic baths or buckets (see tip 25). The work surface on which the dishes have to stand should be covered with some easy-to-clean material such as Formica so that splashes can be wiped up straight away. If possible, the wall behind the tanks should be covered with Formica as well. Finally, of course , it goes almost without saying that dishes should be well washed out after use, dried and put away.

56 The washing tank

When we mentioned washing before (in tips 24 and 25), the point was made that controlling the temperature could be critical in some cases, whether or not the water was running.
However, when washing is being carried out by running water, whether the temperature is controlled or not, there is another point that must not be overlooked. It is important to ensure that the water in the tank does in fact change; in other words you must make sure that the running water does not just pass over the surface, leaving at the bottom of the tank deposits of the very material you are supposed to be washing away. One way round this is to drill a few small holes in the bottom of the tank and set it up on blocks. The water running in from above will then pass through the tank and run out of the bottom, thereby ensuring that the necessary washing action takes place.
There are, of course, tanks you can buy that work on this principle.

57 Notes

It is most important that you keep a notebook handy in your darkroom. There are two ways of making the notes you will need: you can either note the test, with or without the filters, in a book, or note the filters on the back of the print. The first method is suitable if you want to work piece by piece but the second is more convenient if you want to do a lot at once.

The best instrument for taking notes is a good soft pencil, such as the Negro 1 made by Hardmuth. I would advise against using ballpoint or felt tip: if you use resin coated paper (which you'll need) they tend to rub off.

You should be quite meticulous about taking notes every time you do any kind of test. The failures will help you to avoid the same thing in the future.

58 Safekeeping for paper

A good investment in the darkroom is a light-tight bag or box for keeping papers in while the main lighting is on. You will often find the need for this when making test exposures because the piece you have already exposed has to be put somewhere safe while you switch on the white light to set up the next one. This will certainly save you paper but, most of all, it will save you time.

You can buy these at most photo dealers. However, the best way is to make one yourself. A box of 18 × 24 cm ($7\frac{1}{4} \times 8\frac{3}{4}$ in) or 24 × 30 cm ($8\frac{3}{4} \times 12$ in) will be most useful. I made mine with a matt black interior and a flange on the edge to keep out the light. There are, of course, any number of possible designs and, unless you have two left hands, you should be able to make one without any bother.

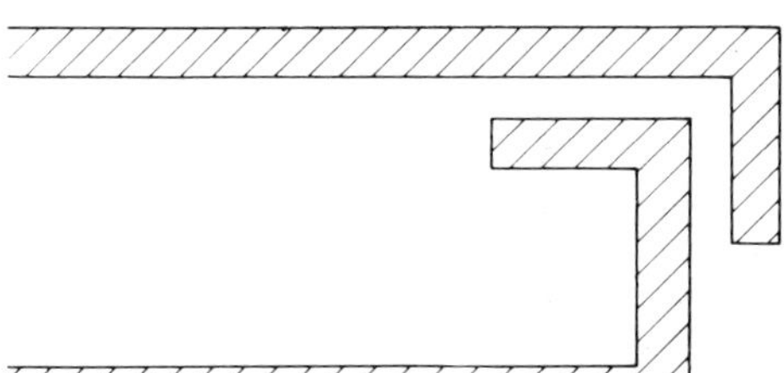

The edge of a light-tight box should look like this

A. A good set of darkroom equipment for colour work (Photo: Agfa-Gavaert)
B. The Agfa-Gevaert colour circle (see tip 3).
C. The extremely compact Durst Colorneg II analyser that fits directly underneath the enlarger lens. This has been replaced by Colorneg III.
D-E. Examples of colour solarization directly on paper: Left – a normal print, Right – solarized with white light (see tip 147).
F. Solarization via a "Positive-M" intermediate negative (see tip 148), made from a black-and-white negative.
G. Ten exposures of the same negative through different filters produced this interesting pattern.

59

Watch your fingers!

You still come across people who feel the need to work in developers with bare hands. Don't be one of them. In the first place, colour developers aren't hand lotions – most of them, in fact, are irritant and the least you'll end up with is brown fingers. In the second place, many of the modern resin-coated papers can easily be damaged when wet by the touch of a bare hand. So, at the very least, you should wear gloves. Even better, in my opinion, is to get into the right habits from the start and use forceps.

These should be made of stainless steel or of plastic. Make sure there are no sharp edges on the tongs otherwise you will get scratched prints. What I do is to rub the edges down gently with fine sandpaper to ensure absolute smoothness. Another way is to use the little rubber or plastic boots you can get to go over the ends.

60

Heating the developer

We've already mentioned heating the washing water but the developer and the other solutions must also be maintained at a constant temperature, sometimes to very fine limits. If you're working at a temperature of, say 18°C, it is theoretically possible to heat the whole darkroom to that temperature and dispense with the need for heating the developer dish altogether. Naturally, this means that the room must be kept at this temperature accurately and this implies the need for thermostatic control – either automatic or monitored by you as you work.

There is another way, of course, and this is to heat the dish itself. One method is a sort of water-jacket arrangement. In a large outer dish, water is maintained at a constant temperature and the developer dish stands on a sort of plateau in the middle of it.

A

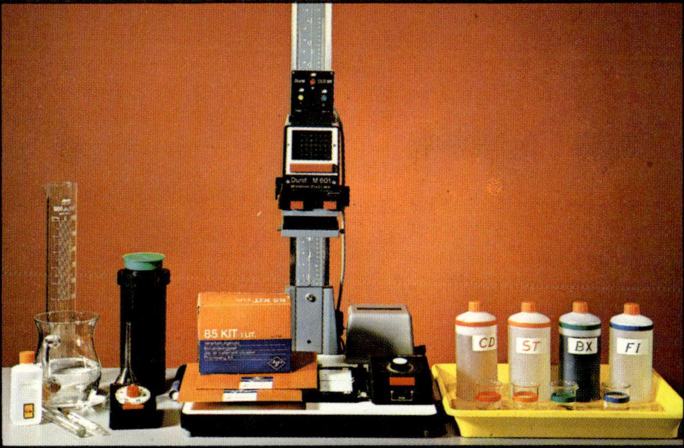
Durst M 601
85 KIT 1 LIT.
CD
ST
BX
FI

B

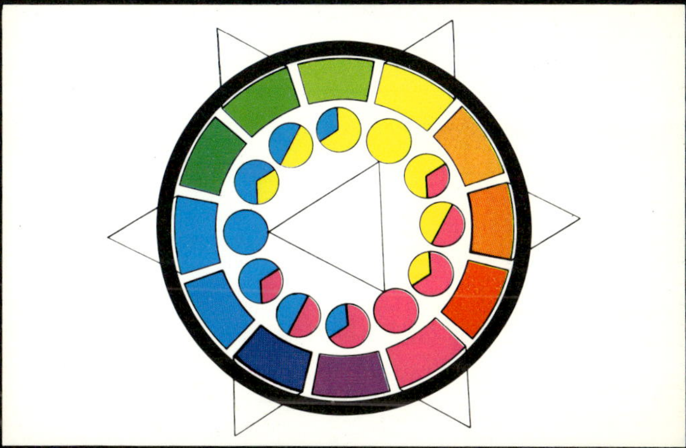

C

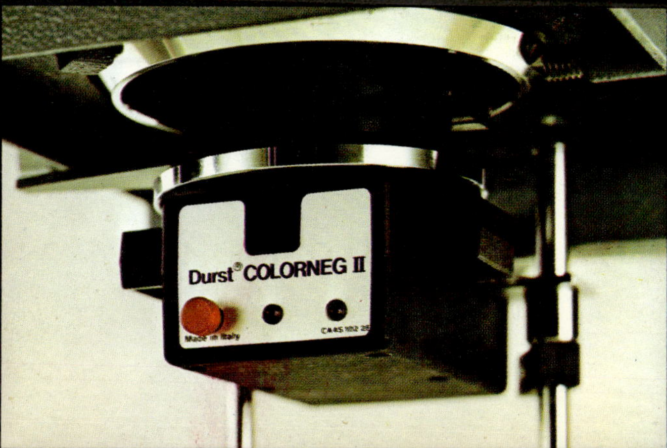
Durst® COLORNEG II
Made in Italy

D

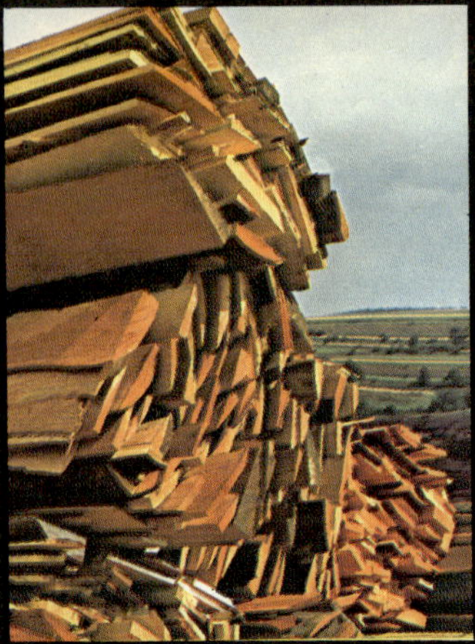

E

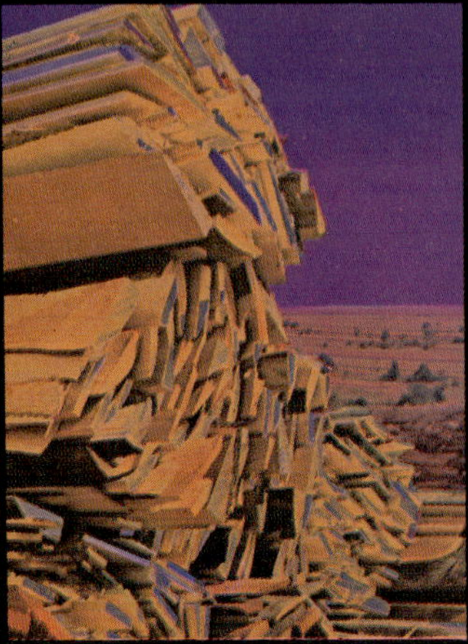

F

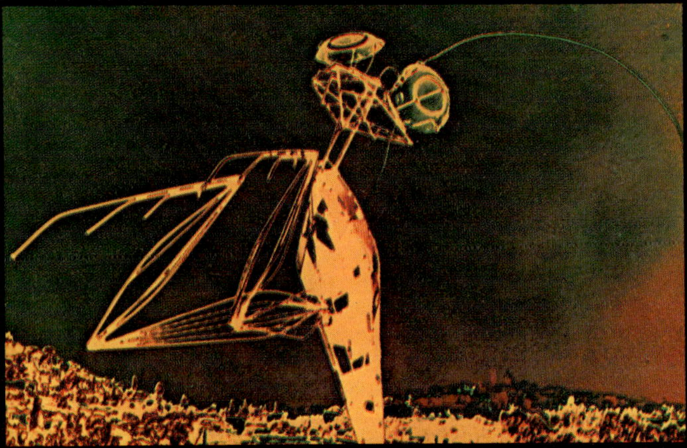

G

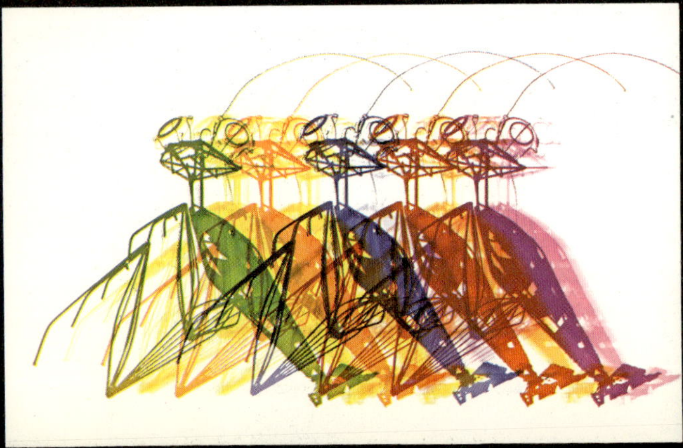

61 **Heating other dishes**

You might well ask whether all this temperature control is absolutely necessary. The answer is that it is if you want to work accurately and get the best results.

However, there are invaluable aids for both tank and dish enthusiasts, namely the Paterson Thermodrum and the Jobotherm. These are strong plastic boxes in which four 250 ml bottles and four measures can be maintained at a given temperature. It seems to me a much better bargain than using four extra heaters if you work with dishes. You simply fill it with warm water a few degrees higher than your working temperature and place it on a low-temperature heater or dish heater.

The Jobo TBE and the Durst Co-temp are similar but have built in heaters and automatic temperature control.

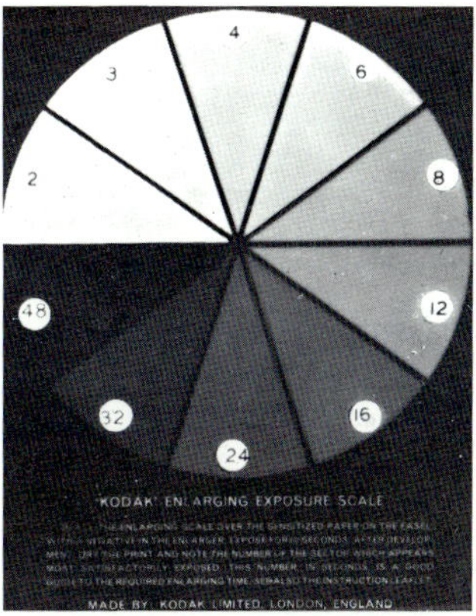

The Kodak enlarging scale

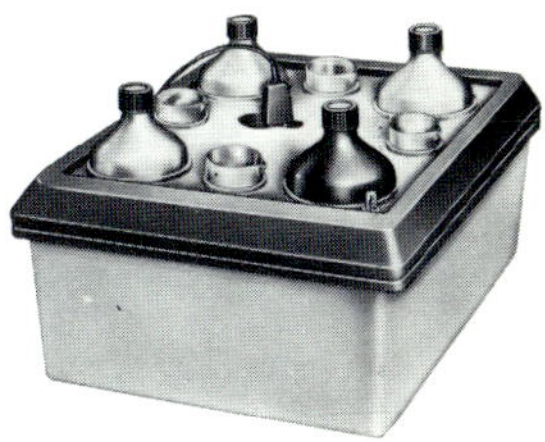

The Jobotherm

62 **The Kodak enlarging scale for colour**

For many years this handy little device has been used in black-and-white work and it is no less useful in colour work. It consists simply of a piece of plastic film with ten grey-tinted segments of increasing density, numbered from 2 to 48. If you don't have a colour analyser you can use this scale to determine your exposure. You can get an accurate result from a test print by using this method. The actual way of using it is as follows:

Without any filters in the enlarger but with the chosen negative in the carrier place a 9 × 9 cm piece of sensitive paper on the baseboard and, with the enlarging scale lying on the paper, expose for 60 seconds. After developing and drying the print, examine it and see which of the segments gives the best result. The number of that segment determines the required exposure in seconds. For instance, if the segment numbered 12 looks best, then an exposure of 10-14 seconds is indicated.

5. Papers

In this set of tips I have tried to set things out in order so that we deal first with the resin-coated papers, then with filter methods, then with developing techniques, and so on.

63

Colour papers

A colour paper emulsion consists of three layers, each one sensitive to one of the primary colours (yellow, magenta and cyan) and colour papers are designed for masked negatives (see tip 13).
These days, the paper itself is sandwiched between two layers of resin which give the relatively rough paper a nice smooth finish. Even these, however, may soon be superseded. Cibachrome-A for example is a colour reversal material for slide printing which is coated on plastic.
These so-called resin-coated papers are given the designation RC which stands for resin-coated.

64

Advantages of resin-coated paper

Before going into the detail of the various types of resin-coated paper, here are some general observations.
These papers in general have a higher sensitivity than the older papers and so are much "faster" in the photographic sense. Because of this they are somewhat more critical as far as exposure times are concerned and so accurate working is essential for good results.
Only very small amounts of fluid material can get through the resin layer, so these papers are very economical on processing chemicals. For the same reason they don't take much washing (two to three minutes is usually enough) and drying is very rapid as well. All of which are points in their favour.

65

. . . . and a couple of problems

These papers do have one or two special points that need attention. They are easily damaged by forceps or similar hard objects. This is especially true at high temperatures: over 25°C they must be handled with extreme care and over 30°C they should be developed only in a tank. So watch out for forceps and fingernails at high temperatures.

Washing and drying require special attention, but we shall have more to say on those subjects in tips 81 and 82. RC papers cannot be dried in ordinary glazers because the resin coating melts at high temperatures.

66

Agfa-Gevaert PE papers

Because Kodak and Agfa-Gevaert are the principal suppliers of colour papers these days, we shall restrict ourselves to their products in this section.

The Agfa designation for their papers is MCN type 5 signifying resin coated paper. The surface finish is specified by another code number interposed between the MCN and the number 5, thus:

MCN 310/5 gloss
MCN 312/5 semi-matt
MCN 317/5 silk finish

67

RC papers for mounting

It has already been pointed out that these papers are sandwiched between two layers of resin. Well, it is possible to remove the back layer, so that the photo can be mounted more easily.

This should be done only when the paper is dry and great care should be taken to avoid cracking the upper surface. The back layer can be peeled off like a skin, leaving the photo somewhat thinner. You should use a glue that is not likely to affect the upper resin surface.

This is especially important if you want to mount several photos on the same surface. I have also tried to peel off the top surface – the one with the picture underneath – but did not succeed. Some of the paper sticks to it, and cracks cannot be avoided. If I'd managed it, of course, it would have made a nice transparency! See tip 199.

68

Kodak RC papers

Kodak papers have the designation Ektacolor 74 RC and are also resin-coated.
There are four types:
RC 74 type F – gloss
RC 74 type N – semi-matt
RC 74 type Y – silk finish
RC 74 type E – lustre-luxe

The smallest available pack is 25 sheets of 8″× 10″ (20 × 25 cm). Smaller sizes are not available but larger sizes are sold in 10-sheet packs.
It is somewhat softer than Agfa-Gevaert papers; but, of course, this is all a matter of taste.

69

Kodak 74 RC paper

There are one or two other points about these papers that are worth a mention here. For instance, Kodak recommend that you use an amber-coloured No 10H or 13 Kodak filter with your safelight provided you keep it at least 1.2 metres (4ft) away from the paper and for not more than 4 mins. You will have to incorporate a Kodak CP-2B UV filter into your pack for processing, but the rest of the filter system is normal.
Kodak recommend the following for a basic pack as a starter but there will be variations from batch to batch:

Durst (dichroic filters)	Kodak CP filters with halogen lamp
Vericolor II 100Y + 60M	90Y + 80m
Kodacolor II 120Y + 60M	110Y + 80M

You will note the high correction in yellow and magenta because of the weak masks in C-II films. You can, of course, use the Agfa ME or Paterson YM filter as a basic correction for this if you wish (see tip 101).

70

Kodak chemicals for 74 RC papers

Kodak market the Ektaprint-3 kit for dish or drum processing at a temperature of 31°C (88°F)
Made-up developer will keep for about six weeks, and bleach-fixer for eight. Both come in fluid form and are available in one-litre packs for the amateur market. Total time per print is about 9 minutes.

Using Ektaprint-3 for Kodak 74 RC paper

Process	**Time (mins)**	**Temperature**
Pre-soak	1	31°C (88°F)
Developer	$3\frac{1}{2}$	31°C ± 0.3 (88°F ± $\frac{1}{2}$°)
Bleach-fix	$1\frac{1}{2}$	31°C (88°F)
Wash	2	31°C (88°F)
Stabiliser	1	31°C (88°F)

Times include a 20-sec allowance for pouring.
Because of the high temperatures processing is better carried out in a tank.

71

Photocolor II for colour prints from negatives

Photocolor II kits have already been described in Tip 37 for processing Type 2 colour negative films. They can be used also for processing colour prints on Kodak Ektacolor 74RC, Sakuracolor and similar resin coated papers, and for this purpose an additive to the colour developer is supplied together with a ml measure. It is actually an accelerator. You can also process Agfacolor Type 4PE paper in which case the additive is not required.

Prints can be developed in drums or dishes (see tip 55) but, for the amateur, drums are preferable because it is not easy to work in dishes in darkness, nor to maintain their correct temperatures. If you do use dishes I strongly recommend you to employ forceps or rubber gloves as some of the chemicals can cause skin irritations.

There are only three baths but if a drum is used it should be preheated for one minute. (See tip 126).

The sequence for Ektacolor 74RC and Sakuracolor is:-

Pre-heating	1 minute
Colour development at 38°C (100°F)	2 minutes
Stop Bath at 38°C (100°F)	10 seconds
Bleach-Fix at 38°C (100°F)	1 minute
Wash in running water at 38°C	1½ minutes
Total Time...	5 minutes 40 seconds

The sequence for Agfacolor Type 4 is:-

Pre-heating	1 minute
Colour development at 34°C (92.5°F)	3 minutes
Stop Bath at 34°C (92.5°C (92.5°F)	10 seconds
Bleach-Fix at 34°C (92.5°F)	1½ minutes
Wash in running water at 34°C (92.5°F)	2 minutes
Total time...	7 minutes 40 seconds

The instruction book gives revised times for processing at lower temperatures. The 1 litre kit will process about 16-25 20 × 25 cm (8 × 10 in) prints, depending on the amount of solution required for the drum in use.

72

Chemicals and processing for Agfa type 4 papers

The Agfa type 4PE paper can nowadays be processed with one of several developers.

You can, of course, get the 85-kit, from Agfa themselves. This is a three-bath system, obtainable in packs of one litre.

The one-litre kit will do about 1 m^2 (approx 11 sq ft) of paper. It contains two one-litre packs of developer, because you need about twice as much of this as of the other solutions. Of course, this means that you will have a litre left over if you work with a drum in which equal quantities are used.

Processing times	at 30°C (86°F)
Developer	2 mins
Wash	½ min
Bleach-fixer	2 mins
Wash	2 mins
Stabiliser	1 min
Final rinse	1½ mins

73 **Stopbath for PE paper**

If you prefer you can use a stopbath instead of the wash between developer and bleach-fix. Mix 76 ml of 80% acetic acid solution with one litre of water, or, alternatively, you can use citric acid in which case you add 40 gm to one litre of water. Either solution, once made up, will keep for about a fortnight. There are also concentrated stop solutions, for example, Acustop and Indicol, available from photo dealers.

74 **Final rinse**

Here, there is some confusion. Agfa-Gevaert call the stabilizer of their 85-kit a "final rinse". Now I am an advocate of stabilizers – they harden the emulsion as well as stabilizing it in respect of light sensitivity. Agfa-Gevaert state that 5 ml of 37% formalin should be added to their "final rinse".

If any other system supplies a stabilizer, I advise you to use it. However, the most recent developments of both Kodak and Agfa seem to omit the stabilizer on account of the altered composition of the other solutions and it is not required with Photocolor II.

75 **Washing resin-coated papers . . . .**

As already noted, washing these papers is only a matter of a couple of minutes. However, in tip 197, I have given one or two notes on some equipment to be used for washing them.

I should also like to point out that washing for longer than the prescribed period is not to be recommended. This is because, first of all, the water seeps through into the paper layers, which slows drying and, secondly, the colours tend to wash out. This shows up as a green cast, because it is the purple layer that washes out first. Mind you this can occasionally be turned to advantage and used as a colour correction. I have had enlargements that came out with too much magenta in them and given them a bit more of a wash to tone it down. It's not exactly a standard technique and you won't find it described in any textbooks, but you can take my word for it.

76 **. . . . and drying them**

There are several ways of drying these papers but a hot glazing press is *not* one of them. This would melt the resin layer which would stick to the glazing drum and make a terrible mess of it as well as the photograph. Some equipment for drying plastic-coated prints is described in tip 199.

You can, of course, simply use a hair-dryer to blow your photos dry or you can lay them out on blotting paper or clean cloth. Paterson make a special squeegee which speeds drying and Durst make an electric print dryer especially for RC papers.

77 **Get developers in quantity . . . .**

There are several reasons why you should buy your chemicals where possible in five-litre packs. You get them cheaper this way, but also you always have plenty of material to hand.

If you want to make large prints a one-litre pack won't go far. A disadvantage might be that you more or less have to make up these five-litre packs at once – I don't recommend splitting them up into smaller units if only because you are unlikely to get the proportions right when you come to mix them up. Actually, it's not too difficult if you get yourself a set of five-litre containers with taps let into them. Then you can make yourself a "chemical bar", and tap off what you need (see illustration).

78 **. . . . and don't be mean with them**

Many amateurs who work in colour – those who use dishes, at least, as opposed to those who use drums – tend to use too little developer, or to keep it for too long.

Just wetting the bottom of the dish, is both pointless and dangerous. You should try to assess how much is needed for an evening's work, and throw it away when you've finished. You can work this out with the help of the data sheet you get with the developing kit – it tells how many prints can be processed per litre.

This is not wasteful but just the opposite. You will find that using too little is false economy and that this technique of estimating as accurately as possible how much developer you need for a session will, in fact, save money. This applies to a lesser extent to the other solutions in the kit, too. These, however, do have a greater capacity and they are not so critical as developer whose function is vital to the success of the whole operation.

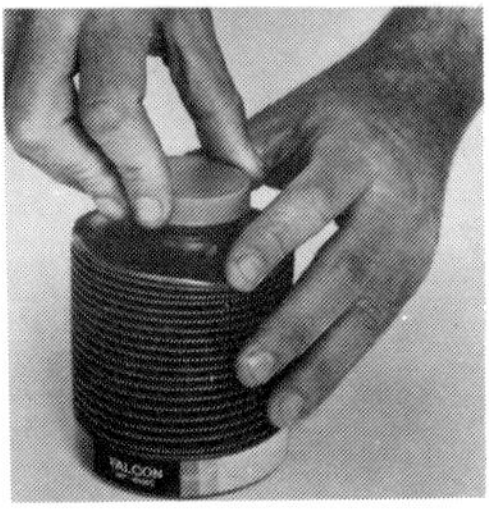

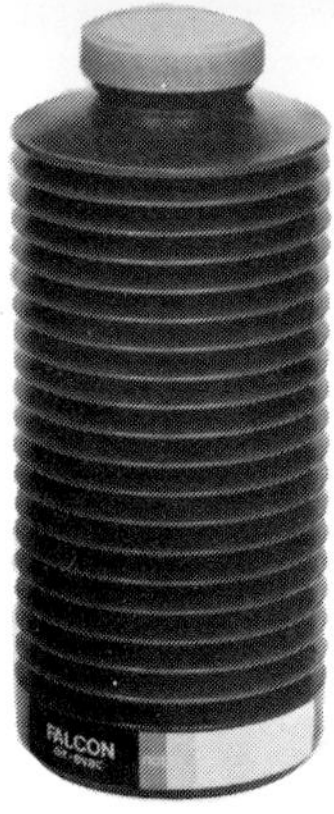

Concertina bottles help to preserve developers.

79 . . . . and keep your eye on them!

The greatest enemy of developers is oxidation which degrades them very rapidly. There are various counter-measures such as splitting a made-up solution between several small bottles filled to the brim to exclude air. Alternatively, there is a spray on the market called Protectan (made by Tetenal), which is a sort of gas that lies on top of the liquid and keeps the air off. Squeeze bottles made like concertinas enable air to be excluded whatever the quantity of solution.

Generally, low temperature is a good protection too. I keep developers as cool as possible, down to 10°C if I can. So, if you can book a corner of the fridge do so. Otherwise, it means finding the coolest room in the house to keep your developers in. It may be the cloakroom; it doesn't matter, though, as long as you don't waste valuable solutions or irreplaceable photographs.

80 Yellow spots

You may find, after the bleach and subsequent washing, that yellow spots appear on the print or that the edges are not completely white, even yellow. In nine out of ten cases the cause lies with the bleach/fixer. As its name implies, this solution has a dual function – bleaching and fixing. The more the solution is used the more it is likely that the bleaching effect will be greater than the fixing effect. Thus the photo is not being properly fixed but is still being bleached. The result is yellow spots or discoloured edges just as with black-and white paper. However, if the colour is all right – indicating that the bleach was still working – all you have to do is to put the print into fresh bleach/fixer, and the yellow stains will disappear.

81

Tetenal high-speed paper processing kits

These are good kits and also very rapid. You use the high-speed PA kit (in fluid form) for all Agfacolor papers, including resin-coated ones, and the PK kit for Kodak RC papers. It is a two-bath system, and it is possible to have a photo out in only two minutes. The kits are available in both one-litre and five-litre sizes. The keeping qualities of the solutions are about average – four weeks for developer and six to eight weeks for the bleach/fixer. There is no need for a stopbath, on Tetenal's own advice. Tetenal don't even recommend a stabilizer but you can get one as an extra. I'd advise you to do so.

82

Colour chemicals for both film and paper

One of the most recent developments in photographic chemicals is the emergence of a kit that can be used for processing both film and prints. This is the Photocolor II pack from Photo Technology Ltd, which comes in fluid form. (See tips 36 and 71)

It can be used for any Type II colour negative film but cannot be used for any of the Agfa films. However, both Agfa and Kodak 74 RC papers can be used with these chemicals.

The made-up solutions can be used first for processing the film and then for paper, but *not* in the reverse order. The kit goes quite a long way: with 20-shot 35mm films you will be able to process 18 films with Photocolor II. For papers, the kit will give about 24 to 35 prints on 20 × 25 cm (8 × 10 in) paper.

Photocolor II has only two baths, but, as the instructions for use advise that a stop bath should be used, you will have to make it up or use either Acustop or Indicol.

83

Using the Tetenal high-speed kit

These high-speed kits are intended specifically for use in developing drums. If they are used properly they can form a two-minute system at 40-42°C (104°-108°F). You don't need to work at these high temperatures, of course, and the table below gives you working times at lower temperatures. I've tried both ways – working at 40°C in a drum as well as at 30°C in a dish, with excellent results in both cases.

With the drum at the recommended working time of one minute at 40-42°C, I found there was a tolerance of ±10 seconds. With the dish, the working time was somewhat longer, about three minutes.

Keeping the bleach at one minute produced a blue cast that wasn't the result of faulty filtering. With a slightly longer developing time, the photos had a good fresh colour.

Tetenal call the stabilizer a "stabilizing and light-proofing solution". It is available in 25 and 250 ml packs.

Working times for the Tetenal PA and PK kits

°C	Minutes	Seconds	°C	Minutes	Seconds
42	1	00	29	3	00
41	1	00	28	3	20
40	1	00	27	3	30
39	1	06	26	3	55
38	1	12	25	4	10
37	1	18	24	4	30
36	1	24	23	4	45
35	1	30	22	5	10
34	1	48	21	5	30
33	2	00	20	6	00
32	2	12	19	6	30
31	2	30	18	7	00
30	2	42	washing at 20°C (68°F) 10 minutes		

84 Paterson Acucolor 3 for colour prints.

This is a print processing kit suitable for Ektacolor RC74 or Fujicolor Type 8907. There are three solutions in the 1 litre kit – colour developer, bleach-fix and stabilizer, and they will process about twenty 20 × 25 cm (8 × 10 in) prints or their equivalent. Storage life of diluted solutions is about 8 weeks.

The following process times are for drum or dish development:-

Colour developer at 31°C (88°F)	$3\frac{1}{2}$ minutes
Bleach-fix at 31°C (88°F)	$1\frac{1}{2}$ minutes
Wash in running water at 31°C (88°F)	2 minutes
Stabilize at 31°C (88°F)	1 minute
Total Time . . .	8 minutes

The temperature of the colour developer is critical to within ±3°C (+$\frac{1}{2}$°F) but there is a 1.5°C (2°F) tolerance with the other solutions. If washing water is not available there should be at least five changes over a period of 10 minutes.

85 Test strips

The life of the amateur colour worker can become a lot easier if he is prepared to make a few test strips. The use of analysers (devices for determining what filters are needed), together with better papers and chemicals, has greatly reduced the need for test-strip making but they are very expensive. Test strips are a rather time-consuming occupation but a little planning can save a lot of sweat. Obviously, making test strips from one negative is inefficient so make a few at the same time from different negatives. You can then easily see which will need further adjustment. Naturally, you do all the developing and further processing at once, to save even more time.

86

Sorting saves time

You can save time when making test strips if you care to sort out your negatives in advance. For instance, photos taken at the same time and under the same conditions will not differ much in printing requirements. It pays to have an orderly approach: making test strips from negatives picked out at random is just a waste of time and paper.

You will save yourself time and effort if you work to a standard set of exposure times such as 5 – 10 – 15 – 20 secs, etc. This means that you don't have to note them down every time and saves you effort there as well. In making your notes try to keep only to the most important details relevant to each photograph.

You can also save yourself a lot of time by using a Paterson printing frame. You put the complete film into this frame and, after having made a couple of test strips as described above, you can make a print showing all of the negatives, which is ideal for reference and filing.

87

Basic corrections

Quite a lot of people prefer to produce a balanced copy first (see tip 95) and then go on to make a fixed correction. You can, of course, get results in this way but an alternative method is to go straight on to use the basic-correction method. I should point out here that certain materials and certain methods of working give rise to colour casts on their own account. Kodak usually quote a basic correction value for their materials. This correction can vary from case to case and from manufacturer to manufacturer; there are no hard and fast rules. This may seem a little complicated on the printed page but in practice you will soon find that you really need the same colour correction. If you use a halogen bulb in the enlarger it will most probably be yellow/magenta by the subtractive method. Once you catch on to the idea, you'll save yourself a lot of time when making test strips.

88

Test strip holders

This is a useful little accessory that can take some of the tedium out of test strip making. It consists of a plastic frame with a sliding cover that can be drawn back gradually to expose, section by section, a strip of photographic paper held inside it. You can make a set of strips and cut them off to length or you can cut them shorter or longer as you wish up to a given maximum. Durst and Tetenal both make strip holders, the former being equipped with magnets that hold it down to a metal baseboard.

The pieces of paper that are exposed are a little on the small side, so I usually go for 13 × 18 cm (5 × 7 in). For larger test pieces I prefer the Durst Comask mentioned in tip 51.

89

Developing test strips

Many beginners make the mistake of treating test strips in a rather cavalier fashion, messing about with processing times and generally regarding them less than seriously. You must get hold of the idea that unless you take your test strip very seriously indeed you cannot expect to get good prints: the whole idea of making a test strip is invalidated unless you give it exactly the same treatment as you intend to give the finished print.

One example of how this mistreatment can happen unintentionally is in noting down the details of the test strips as you put them into the developer. If you have several to do, and you do them one at a time, then of course the last one is going to get a much shorter developing time than the first. So you should make sure that you put them all in together, especially at higher temperatures where the difference of even a few seconds may be noticeable.

90

Beware of artificial light

If you work in the evenings – and most amateurs do – then you will no doubt have to examine the final result of your test strips by artificial light. Some, unthinking, just look at them under an ordinary light-bulb and, because the light from an ordinary bulb is orange-yellow in colour a wrong impression of the colours will be obtained. If you cannot examine your prints by daylight you must get an artificial light source of the same colour temperature as daylight to check them by. There are special fluorescent tubes you can get that are a good approximation to daylight – the 55-57 made by Philips is a good example. Unfortunately, they only seem to come in 120 cm (4 ft) or greater lengths, which is a bit on the big side for a small darkroom.

91

Colour-balanced prints

We could get very technical here but we shall try to avoid doing so. Suffice it to say that a balanced print is one in which a ripe tomato looks red and not purple.

You will generally have a good idea what the photo ought to look like. You will probably remember where it was taken and what the colours were then. Look at the whites and greys – these are colours, too – and see whether they have come out properly. They will show you clearly whether or not there is a colour cast.

92

Colour casts and dominant colours

These terms should not be confused. A colour cast is an error in the colours of a print whereby all colours and tints are affected in the same way and by the same amount. On the other hand, a dominant colour, which at first can give the impression of being a colour cast, is a colour which occupies a considerable proportion of the field of view (green in a nature shot for example) but does not actually alter the other tones in the picture.

The colour reproduction of a photograph is affected by many factors such as the time of day at which it was taken, the age of the film, incorrect exposure, or errors in processing. Since our eyes see all colours more or less accurately at the time of taking the photo it is disappointing to find that the print comes out with something different. It is when this happens that we have to correct it by filtering.

93

Filter designations

The filters we use have well-defined standard designations. For the *subtractive* method, we work with yellow, purple and blue-green filters. These names are, however, "layman's language"; in the photographic world they are called yellow, magenta and cyan. These colours are known internationally by these names and so they are used as initials for filters, thus – Y, M and C. When you specify a set of filters, therefore, you can do it simply in terms of these three letters, followed by a number that represents the strength of a filter for that particular colour, for example Y15 M20 CO. The colours used in *additive* filtering are red, yellow and blue; abbreviations for this method are similar, for example R50 Y20 B40.

94

Filter densities

As you will have noticed in the previous tip, the "strength" or density of the filter is represented by a number that is written after the letter which indicates the colour of that filter. This is what you quote when you want to buy one, or what will be quoted in tables of instructions, etc. Unfortunately, these densities are not standardized and have to be used with filter factors to convert the density numbers of one manufacturer to those of another. Overleaf I have given a conversion table for the three main manufacturers – Kodak, Agfa and Durst. In any given set of filters, of course, the range of numbers will be on the same scale. Paterson make an excellent range of gelatine filters ranging from 0-155Y, 0-155M and 0-75C plus a U.V. filter and a YM at a very reasonable price.

95 **First test print**

All right, you might be saying, we've read all this so far but how do you actually go about doing it? The first thing to do is to make a basic test print which will tell you two things: - the overall exposure time and the principal colour cast or dominant colour. This is made on the test strip principle (see tip 88), without any filters in the drawer (in other words, the filters are Y0 M0 C0. You maxamination of this initial print that there is no need for filters because the print is perfect and has no obvious colour cast of any kind. But, this being an imperfect world, it will happen much more often that a colour cast will be apparent, and that is when you start setting up your filters.

The next step was described in principle in tip 87. It is simply the first correction you make to the plain test print. In fact, the plain print plus the basic correction is the only really neutral copy because the need for a basic correction is built into the material and the enlarger of the system you're using.

96 **Correcting colour casts**

Once you have got this far you are ready to start removing any colour cast there might be. There are two ways of doing this – one expensive and elegant, the other cheap and laborious.

To deal with the expensive method first – what you need is a colour analyser. This is fully explained in tips 178-189, and so will not be described any further here.

The other method is to make a series of test strips, as has been described in previous tips.

By whatever route, you will then have arrived at the necessary colour correction and this will be achieved by means of a pack of filters placed in the filter drawer of the enlarger or by the colour head of your enlarger if you have one fitted (tip 173). This will also be affected by whether you prefer to use the additive or subtractive system. You will, however, find that the latter is the most commonly used.

Filter Density Conversion Factors

Agfa	Durst	Kodak	Agfa	Durst	Kodak
05 15	2.5 7.5	10	80	40	
20 30	10 15	20	110 120	55 60	80
40	20		130	65	
50 60	25 30	40	140 150	70 75	100
70	35	50	160	80	
			170	85	

97

Kodak colour correction filters

Kodak, of course, also produce a range of colour correction filters for use with their 74 RC papers. The filters may be obtained separately, but the complete series consists of three sets of four filters, 75 × 75 mm, for amateurs. There are four densities: 05, 10, 20 and 40. When using this kit with Kodak papers a UV filter must be used, designated CP-2B.

Because the modern 74 RC paper requires a rather high yellow and magenta setting when used with a colour head and halogen lamp it may well be that cyan will not be needed. In this case you can get two extra filters, designated CP-40 Y and CP-40 M or you can use the Paterson 80YM.

Paterson filters

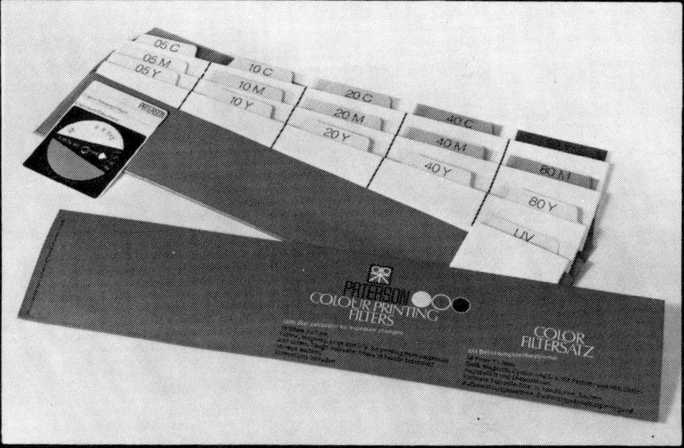

98

Other filter sets

After Kodak and Durst, probably Paterson kits are the most commonly used. They provide a set of 7 × 7 cm filters with a UV and YM filter included.

The Paterson set comes in a plastic case together with an exposure correction calculator. Maximum densities are 155 for yellow and magenta, and 75 for cyan. This set also has a red filter, designated 80 YM which is useful for Kodacolor negatives.

Density values are similar to those for the Kodak kit (see tip 94).

Photo Technology have a set of plastic filters which, unlike Gelatin filters, are washable and heat-resistant.

H. This photo has been used as an "ideal negative" (see tip 192) by the author for many years.

I. Careful use of the analyser makes shots like this easy to print.

J. An affect gained with a trick lens attachment which splits the left-hand side of the print in four while leaving the right-hand side unaltered (the lens is rotatable, so the effect can be done on any part of the picture).

K. Colour print direct from a slide onto Ektachrome RC 14 paper (see tip 157).

99 The Kodak print viewing kit

This is very handy for colour-balance corrections. It consists of a set of cards, each with three transparent filters in the primary colours and their complements: magenta, red, yellow, green, cyan and blue. They have the values of Kodak correction filters but of course these can be converted if necessary by use of the table given with tip 94.

There is a clearly-outlined instruction sheet which tells you how to use these cards to determine which filters you will need to correct the colour balance of a print.

The set can also be used when working with Ektachrome RC14 paper for making prints from reversal film (colour slides). Then, of course, you have to use the complementary colours. This system gives the colour correction but not, of course, the exposure correction. Durst and Beseler also market similar colour print analysis cards.

The Kodak print viewing kit

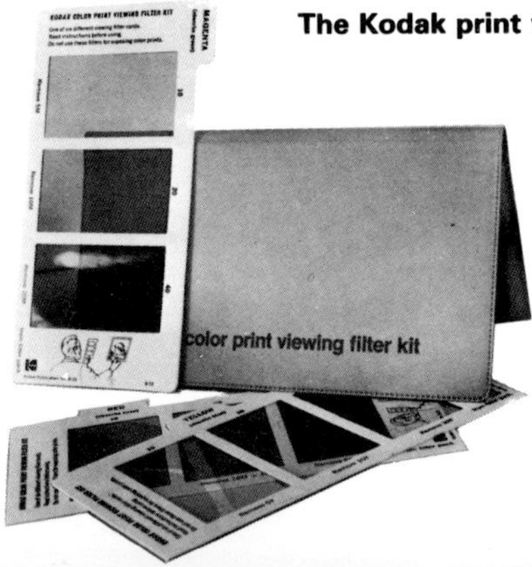

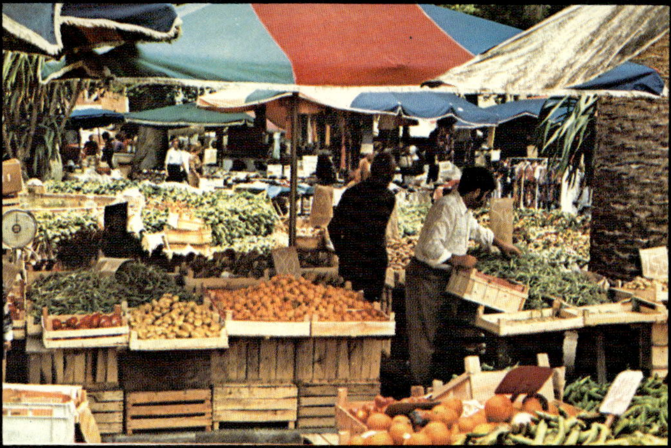

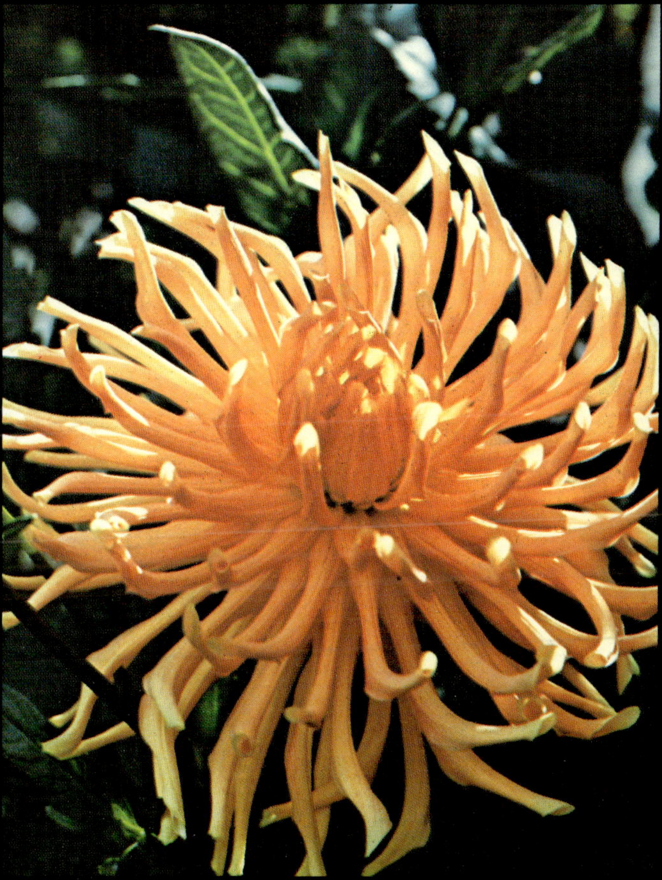

J

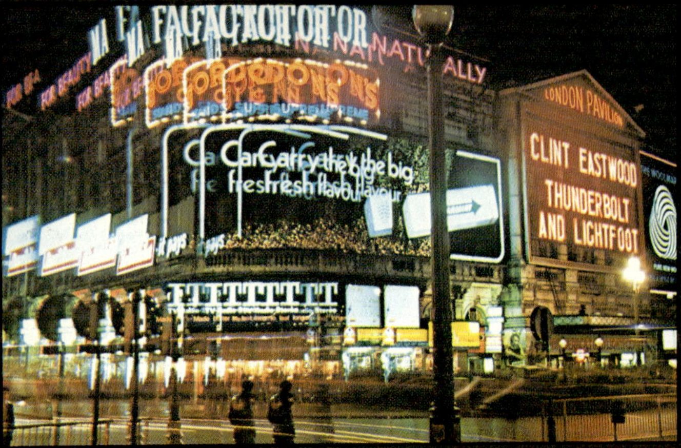
LONDON PAVILION
CLINT EASTWOOD
THUNDERBOLT
AND LIGHTFOOT

K

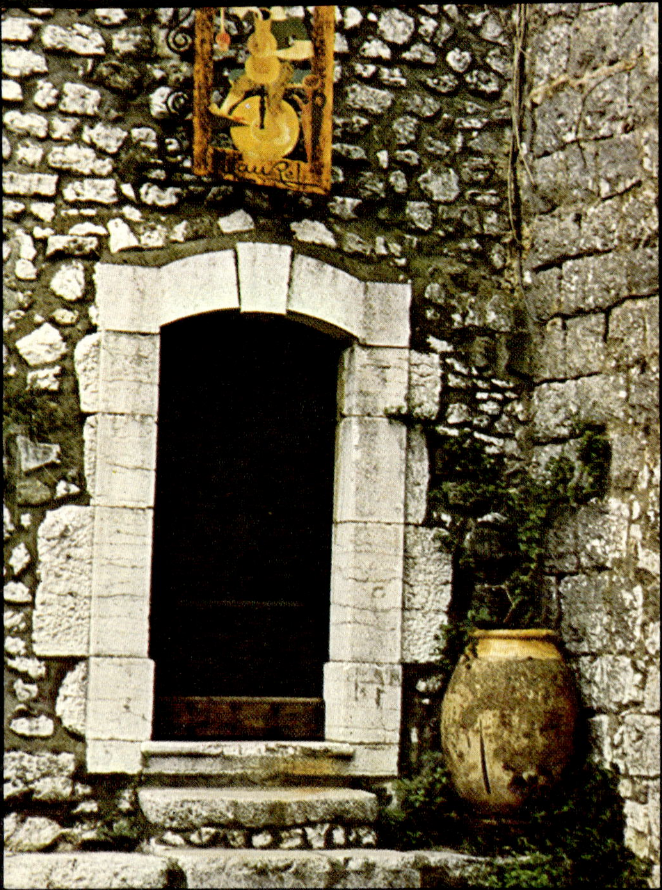

100 **The Agfa-Gevaert ME filter**

This special filter is also a sort of correction filter. It is an orange-yellow filter intended to compensate for masking in colour films. It is therefore used wherever too much yellow and magenta filtering would otherwise be required.

Since the paper that we use at the moment is intended for use with masked films, the lack of such masks produces a colour cast in a print made without mask compensation. Even in the Kodacolor II films, which have weak masks it is still the best solution. You can if you wish just use a high basic correction in yellow and magenta – in Durst values this will amount to Y60 M40. With C-II negatives, the use of an ME filter will cause a cast in the cyan area which will need to be compensated for (see tip 109).

101 **Beseler Subtractive Colour Calculator**

With this system you have a very simple and time-saving method of filter correction which can just as well be used for printing from negatives as it can from slides.

The kit consists of a mosaic of filters in a frame 12 × 10 cm, a diffuser, and a grey card. By using a table supplied with the kit, you can work out from a test print both the exposure time and the amount of filtering required. It can be used with all makes of filter or with a colour head but there are some extra calculations that have to be done.

As you will imagine, this is not quite as good as a colour analyser. However, you will find that with careful use it will give very good results. Particularly with difficult negatives, you will find that there is very little further correction needed.

102 **The Tetenal Filter Calculator.**

This is one of several aids to the determination of correct exposure and filtration in the subtractive process by reading directly from a test print. A diffuser and holder supplied in the kit is attached to the lens which is set at f/8 for 35 mm films or f/11 for 6 × 6 cm films. No filters are used at this stage or, in the case of a colour head, they are set to zero. In total darkness the calculator is placed on a sheet of colour paper not larger than 9 × 12 cm (4 × 5 in) and an exposure of 20 seconds for Kodak 74 RC paper or Agfacolor paper.

After processing and drying the grey comparator is used to find the nearest neutral grey tone. The yellow and magenta filters are then read off on the scales and a series of figures, rather like the old extinction meters, gives the exposure factor. It is somewhat similar in method to the Beseler and the Unicube calculators and it is much cheaper than an analyser. On the other hand, allowances have to be made for different density values between filters of different makes as well as for variations in your enlarger light.

103

Checking correction filters

We have already mentioned that some filters will fade with use and so it is worth your while to find some way of checking them from time to time. You should certainly check the lowest densities once a year at least. Obviously, the 5, 10, and 20 filters get the most use and are therefore most liable to fading. It is of little use to try and check them with the naked eye; you just can't see small changes of colour at those low densities. What you have to do is place the filter in question in the filter drawer, naturally without a negative in the carrier, and make a short exposure on colour paper. You must get the whole filter in so you can make a contact print of the whole filter as a check if you wish, using the enlarger as a light source. You will be able to see in both cases whether the colour is even all over the print. Filters in colour heads, because they are in a dichroic system, don't fade and therefore do not need checking.

104

Printing difficulties with Kodak films

The trouble with Kodak films is that the papers we have at the moment are designed to be used with masked films (see tip 13), which means that very high corrections are needed in the yellow and magenta sectors when using Kodacolor II or Vericolor II. This, of course, requires high densities in the yellow and magenta region of your filter pack to get rid of the red cast. But, as we said in tip 100, you can always use a basic correction or an ME filter. In this respect, the extra red YM filter in the Paterson kit is most useful. With some negatives, however, use of these red filters can cause trouble in the cyan range. This is especially true in the case of photographs taken in the afternoon when the light is redder.
The solution to these problems can only come from Kodak seeing that Agfa are still producing masked films. The problem is not so marked with Kodacolor 400.

105

Printing Kodak films with an ordinary enlarger lamp

The correction methods described in the previous tip can be applied to Kodak film in order to overcome this problem of the lack of masking and both methods have their advantages. However these methods are more likely to be used by those who have a halogen lamp in their enlarger coupled with a colour head. For those who use an older type of enlarger with an ordinary tungsten bulb, however, the colour temperature of the light it gives out will lie much more in the yellow-red range and the use of an ME filter will therefore give far too high a correction. If, on the other hand, you leave out the ME filter you have to remember to make a suitable adjustment in the yellow-magenta filtering. The real problem, of course, is with the paper and until that is cleared up we shall continue to have trouble.

106

What next?

Right! You've made your first test print, with or without a basic correction, and determined what the colour cast or dominant colour is. So what now?

If you use the subtractive method, with either a filter pack or a colour head, (but without a colour analyser, of which more later), then the next thing is to determine what filters to use. This can be quite difficult to begin with but it's no trouble really. Whatever you do, you must remember the first rule of subtractive filter-work: *use a filter the same colour as the cast you want to remove.* So, for example, if there is a yellow cast to the photograph use a yellow filter. This is the most important of all the things you have to learn about filtering. There are only a couple of major rules and they are given in the next few tips. Follow them and you will have no bother in getting the best results from your work.

107

More filter rules . . . .

The second rule you must remember is that colours that don't come into the set of filters can be made up of combinations of them. So green is made up of cyan and yellow, red of yellow and magenta, and so on. You work out these combinations by using the colour circle (see tip 3 and illustration B).

Quite often a colour cast is in fact a combination of two colours, although this may not be obvious at first. Suppose, for example, that there is a reddish cast to a photo. The nearest colour is orange, so start off with that. I would advise you always to start with only one colour – more can be confusing. So now you would have a filter pack made up as Y20 M0 C0. The next proof may then err towards the magenta, which you would then correct, perhaps ending up with a 30Y 25M filter pack.

You should note here that it is rarely that three colours will be needed in the filter pack. Three equal value filters add up to grey because they absorb the whole spectrum equally.

108

. . . . and still more

As we were saying at the end of the previous tip you should not have three filter colours in the pack. If by chance you do end up in this way, and it can happen, then you must realize that the smallest value filter can be removed, so long as you also remove equal values in the other two colours. All you are removing in total is grey.

If for instance you had a combination	20Y, 50M, 10C
then, removing values equal to the lowest from all three	10Y, 10M, 10C
we are left with a final pack which has exactly the same effect!	10Y, 40M.

The strength of the colour cast obviously has a determining effect on the numerical value of the filters you will choose. If a cast looks strongly coloured, go for a fairly dense filter. A noticeable green cast will probably need at least 25Y, 0M, 25C filter set to correct it. On the other hand you have to watch out for overcompensating, which is another problem.

109 **Overcompensation**

It can happen that, if you have a pretty strong colour cast, you might over correct – in other words, put an even stronger filter than necessary into the drawer. What happens then is that you will get another cast, but of the complementary colour. This can sometimes be confusing, and leave the amateur wondering what to do next, but it is really only a matter of knowing your colour circle.
Suppose, for example, you have a photo with a strong purple cast to it, which you then proceed to filter with a 0Y, 50M, 0C pack. When you develop it, horror of horrors, it comes out green! Don't panic. Remember your colour circle. Green is the opposite or complement of purple, so all you have done is been a little too heavy on the magenta filtering. If you just reduce it to 0Y, 45M, 0C or perhaps 0Y, 40M, 0C, you will probably get a perfect result.

110 **Exposure times in filtering**

Another rule of filtering is that filters increase exposure times and naturally the denser they are, the longer the increase in exposure that will be necessary to compensate for them. For example, for yellow filters, increase the exposure by 5% for every ten units on the Agfa scale and, for magenta and cyan, by 10% for every ten Agfa units. This takes the filter factors into account. So, for example, if your exposure without filters is worked out as eight seconds and you find that you need filters as 0Y, 20M, 30C, then you would work it out as follows: 2 × 10 magenta = 20%; 3 × 10 cyan = 30%; total 50%. Therefore the increase in exposure required is half the originally indicated time, or 4 sec, and the new exposure time will be 12 sec. This rule is not exact but you will find it pretty good for making test exposures without an analyser. The last exposure will enable you to make a final correction before you make the proper print.

111 **Paper factors**

On each pack of colour paper, from whatever manufacturer, you will see what appears to be a filter pack designation, for example – 70Y, 30M, 0C. This is a basic correction for the paper and is the filter value required to make a neutral grey print. If you don't use an analyser this will not mean a lot to you, except when you change to another type of paper with a different basic correction while you are in the middle of a print run. Then you will need to alter your filter pack to take account of the change in paper characteristics. There is a rather complicated method for working this out precisely or you can do what I do – make another test exposure: it's quicker! It's not too difficult to see where the correction is going to come – if the old pack is 70Y, 30M, 0C and the new one is 60Y, 20M, 0C, then the new test exposure is going to need rather less yellow and magenta. My experience is, however, that a change of ten units doesn't have much effect.

112 **More about paper factors**

One or two more points about paper factors. Obviously, the best way of avoiding trouble with paper factors is to make sure you have plenty of the one kind of paper. So, instead of buying packs of ten sheets, get packs of 50 or 100. It will save you bother with filters and it could work out cheaper, too. All colour paper should be stored in a cool place or in a refrigerator. In the latter case take it out at least 4 hours before use.

With some types of colour analyser the paper factors must be fed in with each change of paper.

113 **Uniwheel-Uniguide**

I've already mentioned that, if you must use the *additive* method, there is a system on the market that solves at least some of the problems involved in it. This is the Uniwheel which has three additive filters in a wheel, together with diffuser. There is also a fifth hole that is simply open. The whole assembly is mounted on the lens-holder of the enlarger and the wheel can then be rotated to bring the three coloured filters or the open hole of the diffuser under the lens in turn. A calculator is supplied with the wheel and the test exposure is made through the diffuser. The required filtering can be worked out after the test exposure has been developed.

The Uniwheel on a Durst M 605 enlarger.

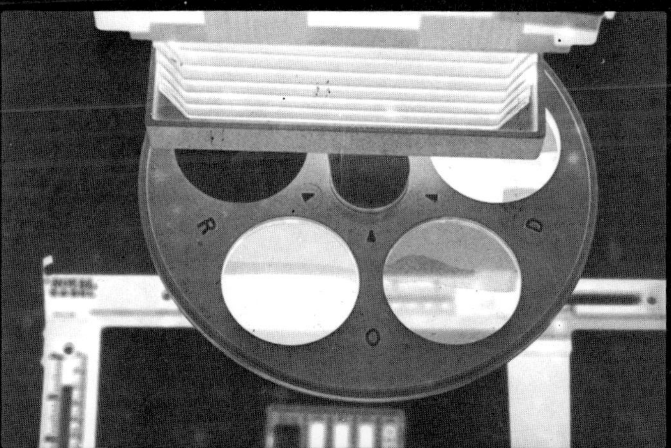

114 The Beseler Calculator

A similar system is available from Beseler and this consists of a simple diffuser which is placed under the lens after the negative has been focused. A piece of printing paper approximately 4 × 5 in (10 × 12 cm) is then placed on the baseboard with the Beseler calculator on top of it. The lens should be stopped down to f/11 and an exposure (without filters) of 45 seconds is given. The paper is then processed in the usual way and dried thoroughly. This is necessary because significant colour and density changes can occur as the print dries. It will look something like the illustration below but in colour, starting with blue in the bottom left hand corner through to a magenta/yellow mixture at the top right hand corner. There is also a row of numbers of varying density appearing at the bottom.

115 Checking the test print

The lowest number which is fully formed and easily readable is the correct white light exposure in seconds. There will be a cluster of greyish squares somewhere in the chart and you look for the purest grey. A comparator is supplied to help you with this. The number on it is the filter factor and the white light exposure is multiplied by this to obtain the correct printing time at the aperture used for the test. You now read upwards from the grey square and the last square at the top gives the yellow filtration to use. Similarly, reading from the grey square to the right hand edge gives you the magenta filter to use. If the grey square is on either edge, no filter of that colour is required.

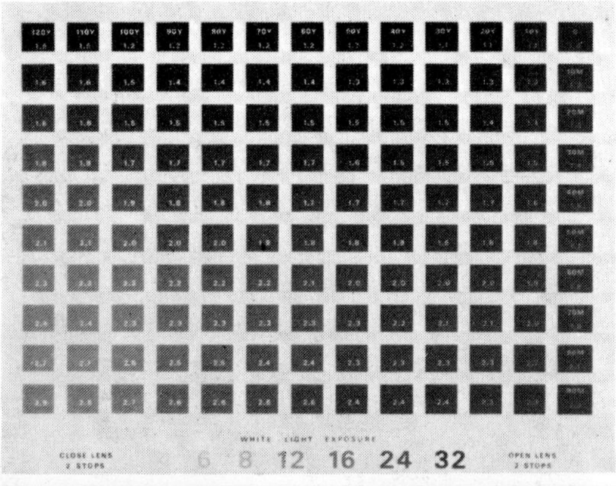

116

Subtractive processing without a filter drawer

I have remarked previously that if you have one of the older enlargers without a filter drawer you will have to use the additive process with filters held underneath the lens.

However, Kodak nowadays make CP filters (see tip 97) as well as CC filters. These optically-corrected gelatin filters are specially designed for use under the lens with the subtractive process. You can knock up some sort of tray to hold them in place and you have a perfectly workable system. The CC filters come in only the three main colours, and don't have the extra red set as the CP filters do. The CP-2B must be used with them, though. It is best if you can arrange for this filter to be placed between the lamp and the negative if you can, rather than below the lens.

The CC filter kit contains the following filters:

Yellow	**Magenta**	**Cyan**
CC025Y	CC025M	CC025C-2
CC05Y	CC05M	CC05C-2
CC10Y	CC10M	CC10C-2
CC20Y	CC20M	CC20C-2
CC30Y	CC30M	CC30C-2
CC40Y	CC40M	CC40C-2
CC50Y	CC50M	CC50C-2

117

More about "under-the-lens" systems

With additive systems you cannot possibly do anything like dodging or burning-in and there are several other problems as well. Not least of these is the fact that filters used under the lens must be handled with extreme care. In the enlarger filter drawer the filters lie outside the focal range of the lens and so any scratches or finger marks will not be projected. With under-the-lens work the least mark on the filter can ruin your photograph and you can't even protect them by mounting them in glass because the diffusing effect of the glass would tend to cause a loss of sharpness in the projected image.

118 **Paper – gloss, matt or textured?**

The papers supplied by most of the big manufacturers come in a choice of surface finishes (see tip 68). Ultimately, whether you like gloss, matt or textured finishes is a matter for your personal taste. However, there is a certain rational basis for choice and perhaps the following remarks will help.

There is no doubt, for example, that a photo printed on gloss paper has a much greater brilliance than either matt or textured finishes. A well-finished glossy photograph will always make a greater impression because of the more brilliant finish it gives. Printers prefer it for reproduction.

Also, although I know there is a terrific amount of silk finish paper being used at the moment I am still convinced that this is a fashion which will disappear. For these reasons I would advise you to work mainly on glossy paper, with matt or fancy finishes being the exception rather than the rule. On the other hand I have to admit that this is at least in part because I like glossy paper, so it is quite possible that others will advise you differently.

119 **Black-and-white prints from colour negatives**

If you're thinking in terms of making black-and-white prints from your colour photographs, I would advise you to use only Kodacolor II or Vericolor II. The difficulties that arise in the making of black-and-white prints from colour films come entirely from the presence of orange masks and, since this type of film has little masking effect, it is certainly the one to use. I have had excellent results with it.

Because of its very dense masking, Agfa-Gevaert CNS film is not very good in this respect. The only way to get reasonable prints from most negative films is to use Kodak Panalure paper, which must be processed entirely in the dark because it is sensitive to all colours.

120 **Difficulties with darkroom production lines**

It can happen that if you are making a series of prints from one negative – for example, if you are making 50 or so prints for a Christmas card – here and there you will find one that is not quite as good as the others, a little lighter or darker.

One of the main reasons for this is the slight variations in temperature that occur when eight or ten prints are done in the dish together. Also, when using only one litre of developer the first photographs processed may come out slightly better than the last ones.

If you're going to do a lot of this it might be as well to invest in a large developing drum. The Jobocolordrum 4102 is the sort of thing you need; in this, you can do four 18 × 24 cm (whole plate) sheets at once. If, by using a Comask, you can make four 9 × 12 cm prints on this you will be able to process your photos sixteen at a time, thereby keeping the quality constant.

With only three operations you have 48 greetings cards!

6. Developing drums

Because of the enormous growth in the use of developing drums for prints in recent years, I thought this subject merited a section of its own.

121 **Print developing drums**

If you don't already know, these are simply tanks, similar to the ones you develop films in, but modified for use with printing paper. They all have their different details such as ways of filling, holding papers, etc, but it is their many advantages over the dish methods of processing which have caused the enormous increase in their use.

122 **Why drums, anyway?**

I mentioned advantages in the tip above. Let us list all the pros and cons and see just what they are.

Advantages:

1. Small quantities of chemicals needed.
2. High quality ensured because chemicals are used once only.
3. All processing, apart from loading, can be carried out in daylight.
4. Very fast methods (high-temperature) can easily be used.
5. Wide choice of systems, materials and accessories.

Disadvantages:

1. Time-consuming in that each photo must be processed individually.
2. Chance of marks on print if drum is not handled properly.
3. Relatively high cost of drums and materials.
4. Manual rolling can be tiring although this can be eliminated by using a motor agitator like the Beseler or Jobo.

123 Using a developing drum (1)

If you take a glance through the "advantages" list in the previous tip you will get a pretty good idea of the method of operation of a developing drum used for prints. All drums use the minimum of chemicals – a little bit more or less depending on the size of the drum, but to give you some idea, a drum large enough to handle 18 × 24 cm prints (8 × 10 in) will use about 60 to 85 ml. The materials are used once only.

The actual method is quite simple. When you have made your exposure, you put the sheet of paper into the drum in darkness, close the lid of the drum firmly and then put the lights on. So for a start you don't need to sit in the dark for long periods of time. The drum is then held in the vertical position while the developer is poured in, after which it is laid on its side so as to distribute the fluid evenly throughout the print. It is then agitated by being rolled back and forth. The Beseler and Unicolor drums have a pouring lip so the drum is placed on its side to receive the solution which passes over the print only when it is rolled.

124 Using a developing drum (2)

The agitation process is the reason why you can use such small amounts of chemicals in these drums. To ensure the maximum distribution of material throughout the drum, it is usually arranged so that the drum moves up and down as it is rolled backwards and forwards by having eccentric end caps.

Rapid methods using high temperatures are possible because, among other reasons, you don't have to handle the paper while the emulsion is soft. However, at these higher temperatures you must be even more careful to ensure a good distribution of developer through the tank, otherwise marks will form on the finished print (see tip 129).

At the end of the process the print is taken out of the drum and washed just as in the dish method. It is usually neither possible nor desirable to attempt to do this in the tank.

125 Which drum?

There are many different makes of drum available nowadays, and no doubt there will be even more in the future. It is therefore difficult to recommend any particular make.

There are no bad drums, so personal preference comes into the choice. My own preference is for the Jobo and so I recommend this, not because I have shares in the company but because I have used many different types and for me the Jobo tank is about the easiest and handiest to use and gives the best results.

There are others, of course. Durst make a good one for 18 × 24 cm and 20 × 25 cm formats and Unicolor produce several of their so-called Unidrums. These makes are also used a great deal, and they also have very good systems keeping the paper in place inside the drum. The Beseler is similar to the Simmard and the Unidrum but by far the most popular in the UK is the Paterson which is made in two sizes – 10 × 8 in and 15 × 12 in and they are cheaper since they are made in Britain.

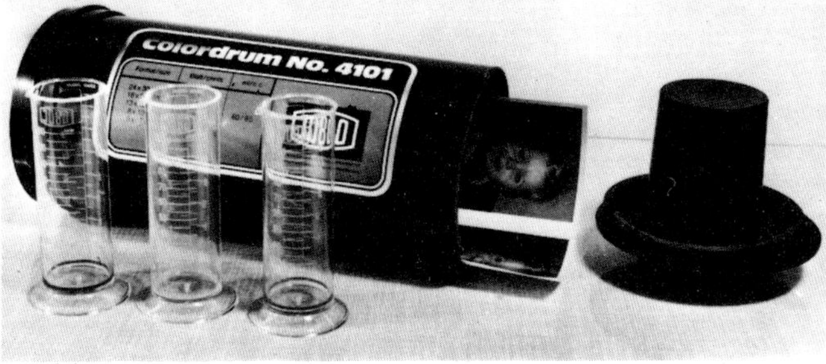

The Jobo colour drum with three measuring glasses.

Using the Simmard drum with preheat

The Simmard drum is used with what is described as a pre-heating system after the paper has been loaded. All this means in practice is that the drum is filled with water warmed to the prescribed temperature or a little above, allowed to stand for one minute and emptied. Here is a table that tells you what temperature to use.

Required processing temperature	Room temperature 15°C	20°C	25°C	30°C
−38°C	—	49°C	47°C	44°C
−36°C	50°C	43°C	41°C	40°C
−34°C	46°C	40°C	38°C	37°C
−32°C	42°C	37°C	35°C	34°C

Based on using 250 ml of water in a 10 × 8in drum.

Naturally, you can use a preheating system with other tanks. Simply fill the tank of your choice with one litre of warm water of the appropriate temperature, and leave it for one minute before emptying and then pouring in the developer.

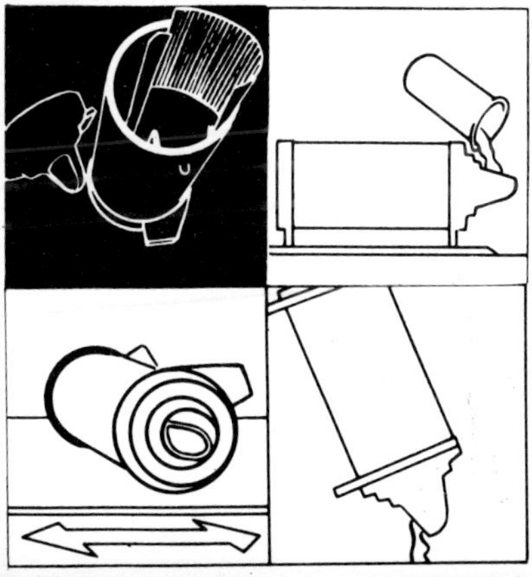

Beseler, Chromega, Simmard and Unicolor drums have pouring lids to hold solutions until they are turned over.

127

Simmard or Unidrum

Drums of this type have a different way of filling and distribution of the fluids used in processing. The drum has a pair of legs on which it stands horizontally while the fluid is poured in through a sort of spout in one end, and comes in contact with the paper when the rolling process begins.
Personally, I doubt the wisdom of pre-washing with resin coated paper in the drum, because this paper takes up so little water that there seems little point. Also, the drum can just as well be pre-heated without paper in it. If you do it quickly it makes no difference and the wet walls are no trouble. This is a way of avoiding what I think is a danger of marks being formed on the print through pre-soaking when using resin coated papers.

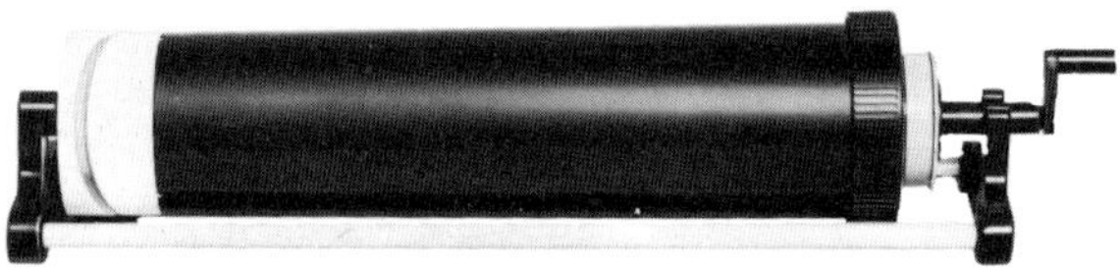

One of the Paterson developing drums with a handy turning gear. They also make one called a Thermodrum which can be turned in a heated water bath.

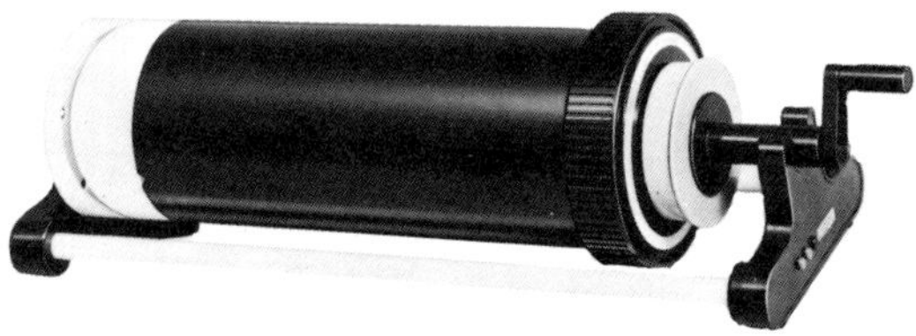

128

The Paterson colorprint drum

This is a very convenient piece of apparatus because it has a handle mounted on one end. The whole drum fits into a special rack in which it is turned by the handle to give not only rotary but also a sideways motion.
The drum is filled vertically and the fluid is held in a reservoir until the drum is moved to the horizontal position when the fluid is distributed over the paper by the rolling action of the drum. There are two sizes, 18 × 24 cm (8 × 10in) and 24 × 30 cm (11 × 14in). By using separators, smaller formats can be treated, as can test strips up to 13 cm long. I particularly like this type of drum for the way in which it avoids the tedious business of having to roll a drum over and over on a table, especially if you are limited for space in your darkroom. Considering the relative complexity of the system, the price is very reasonable.

129 **Work quickly!**

When you pour the liquid in with the drum standing in the vertical position it just goes into a reservoir. But, as soon as you tip the drum over on to its side the solution is released into the drum and begins to spread out over the paper. For this reason you should start rolling the drum as soon as you tip it over, and this is especially true at higher temperatures.

I've heard many complaints at one time or another about drum-developed prints having darker, irregular-shaped areas. What has happened is that the developer has been allowed to stand on the surface of the sheet of paper for a few seconds while our less-than-careful darkroom worker fiddled with something else. During that time the developer was working more on that area than on others; hence the dark mark. So my advice to you is to get rolling immediately the drum is tipped over. And the higher the temperature, the quicker you've got to be.

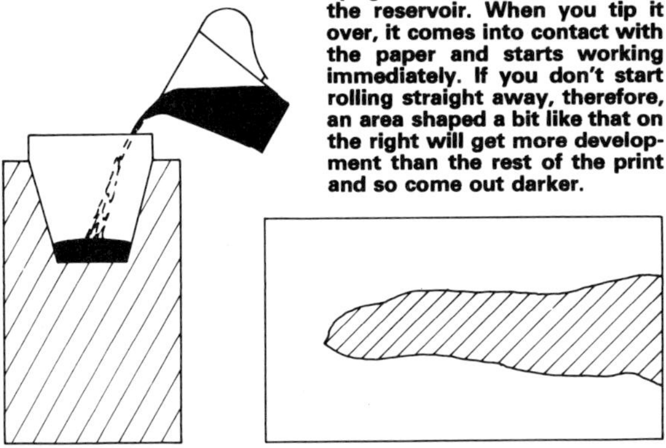

As long as the drum stands upright, the solution remains in the reservoir. When you tip it over, it comes into contact with the paper and starts working immediately. If you don't start rolling straight away, therefore, an area shaped a bit like that on the right will get more development than the rest of the print and so come out darker.

130 **Different sorts of paper holders**

Here I'm referring, of course, to the way that papers are held in place inside the drum. They are located with the picture side facing towards the centre and are firmly fastened down by various sorts of rail or slide into which the paper is pushed when it is being loaded. Different manufacturers have slightly different methods of doing this and some have also made provision for using papers of smaller format than the maximum for which the drum is intended. In all cases, the separators which are provided are there to prevent the papers moving around inside the drum while processing is taking place. However, you must make sure that you put them in the right way – two 13 × 8 cm pieces in an 18 × 24 cm drum will go, but you have to get the 18 cm edges together. Test strips might be difficult, too, because they are usually longer than 18 cm. However, Jobo have put a test-strip holder on the market and Durst and Paterson also make provision for several smaller sizes of paper.

131

Developing Kodak 74 RC paper in a drum

If you want to do high-temperature processing of Kodak 74 RC paper in your developing drum, and you want to use Kodak's own chemicals I'd advise you first of all to use Ektaprint 300 developer. The other chemicals can be the normal Ektaprint 3 type. As we've already remarked, Ektaprint chemicals are supplied in one-gallon packs. However, Ektaprint 300 is available in a 1.9 litre double pack. This is, of course, an important consideration in view of the very small amount of chemicals used in drum processing.

Solution	Remarks	Temp	Time
1. Presoak	In a dish of water	21 - 39°C	½min.
2. Developer		37,8 ± 0,3°C	2 min.
3. Washing	Running water	37,8 ± 1°C	½min.
4. Bleach/fixer		37,8 ± 1°C	1 min.
Room lighting can now be switched on			
5. Washing	Running water	37,8 ± 1°C	½min.
6. Stabilizer	Do *not* wash afterwards	37,8 ± 1°C	½min.
7. Drying	Do *not* glaze	max. 107°C	

132

Developing Agfa PE papers in a drum

Just as with other makes, Agfacolor PE also gives excellent results with drum processing. You should use the Agfacolor 85 kit for it. However, you will find that as long as Agfa-Gevaert continue not to provide separately-available solutions, you will have some difficulty because the chemicals are used once only and you are left at the end with one litre of developer. In the one-litre kit there is a double one-litre pack of developer so it is better to get the five-litre pack.

Process	**24°C (77°F)**
Pre-wash	1 min
Developer 85 CD	5 mins
Stopbath	2 mins
Washing	2 mins
Bleach/fixer (Blix)	4 mins
Washing	3 mins
Final rinse	2 mins

133 The Tetenal high-speed colour kit

It consists of a "mini-processor", a test-strip holder, and a kit of chemicals.
The mini-processor is a small developing drum for 10 × 15 cm (4 × 6in) format and with a holder to make for test strips. The measuring beakers provided hold the right amounts of chemicals (about 35 ml). There is also an extension piece which allows you to work up to 13 × 18 cm (5 × 7 in) and in this case the capacity is 45ml.
This little drum has a double wall with a small ridge to hold the paper. The bottom of the drum bulges out a little (see diagram), and has a filling-spout, which is provided with a rubber stopper.
When the paper has been loaded and the developer poured in, the drum is agitated, not by rolling but by being inverted (see diagram).

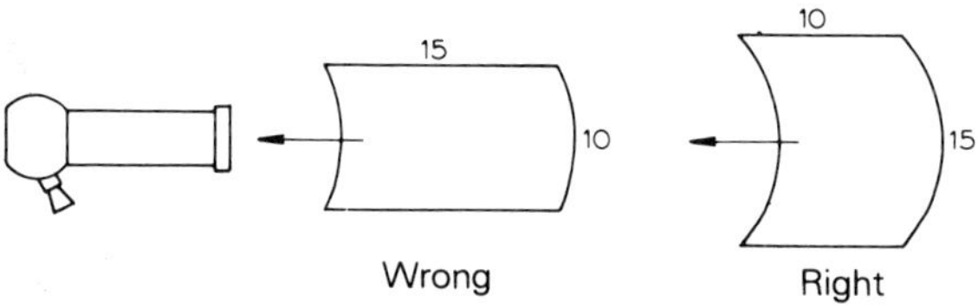

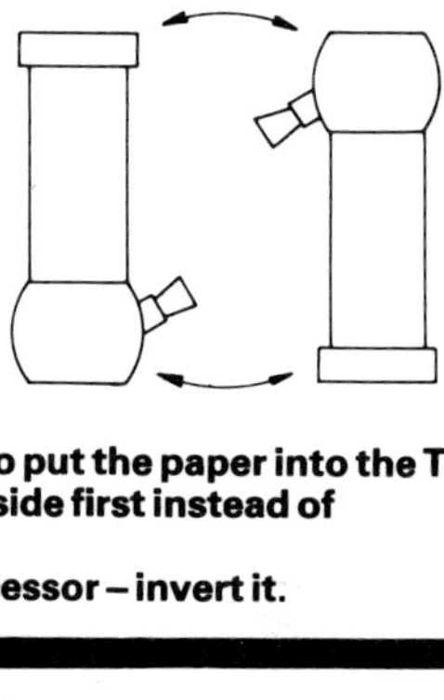

Above: **There is only one way to put the paper into the Tetenal mini-processor – wide side first instead of lengthways.**
Right: **Don't roll the mini-processor – invert it.**

134 The Paterson Thermo-drum

For those who find temperature control difficult but cannot afford one of the expensive automatic processors like the Durst or the Jobo CPE, I can recommend the Paterson Thermo-drum. It does not automatically control the temperature but it makes it easy for you to do so.
It consists of a plastic tank which holds 3 plastic bottles for the solutions and 3 plastic measures, all of which are held in position and not allowed to float about, even when empty, by means of ingenious clips. The developing drum fits into holders at each end, one of which contains a filler and the other a crank for turning the drum. When the tank is filled with water at a few degrees above the working temperature the drum will be partly immersed and turning it will give even development at the right temperature. This is maintained by adding hot water when the temperature drops and at the same time releasing some through the outlet provided.
The cost is about £34 for the 20 × 25 cm (8 × 10 in) print size and £40 for 30 × 38 cm (12 × 15 in). The drum is included in the price.

135 **A warning!**

As with film tanks, you must thoroughly wash and clean your drum when you have finished with it.

A fault that can arise if you don't is that you will get a very bluish print coming out of the drum. This is almost certainly due to a drop of bleach/fixer remaining in the filler spout. This one drop can ruin the whole of the small quantity of developer that you use in a drum, with disastrous results. So take care!

136 **A final word . . . .**

In many of the tips I have referred to the so-called "warm" methods of developing. I should not like you to get the idea, however, that unless you work at 38°(100°F) or above you are some sort of photographic freak.

Perhaps, then, a warning about high-temperature methods would not come amiss, here at the end of this section. You may well have seen it elsewhere in these tips but let it be re-iterated:–

The most important thing about working at higher temperatures is accuracy. Everything you do is absolutely critical –temperature, time, agitation, everything. And all to save a few minutes! So, if you aren't in any particular hurry why stress yourself in this way and take the risk of spoiling your photographs? Take your time and you'll probably end up with much better results. After all, both Tetenal and Agfa recommend their basic working temperature as 25°C.

137 **. . . . and an even more final word about automation!**

If you really want to get automated and get regular quality with the greatest of ease, then the Durst RCP-20 auto-developing system is the one for you. This is a completely automated processing system intended for the advanced amateur or the studio photographer who does his own finishing. The only operation that has to be done in the dark is the loading of the paper. After that, the machine works away on its own and produces – seven minutes later – a print which only needs washing and stabilizing. The next photo can be put in the machine during this seven-minute processing time, and the total capacity of the machine is 20 sheets of 20 × 25 cm (8 × 10 in) per hour.

The machine has a constant throughput, and the process is controlled by means of the temperature, which is given by Durst for most of the best-known processing systems. Maximum format is 20 × 25 cm (8 × 10 in) and minimum is 7 × 10 cm (2¾ × 4 in). One disadvantage is that there is a lot of cleaning to do after a session.

7. Effects and experiments

Once you've mastered the principles of photographic work you can take it from me that you are unlikely to be content with that – merely plodding on with run-of-the-mill processing. In that case, this group of tips will give you some insight into the range of other things you can do. But even then you should remember that these are just a sample – a stimulus to make you look further.

138

Some remarks on experimenting

I can well imagine that there are some readers to whom many of these tips are old hat (hopefully not *very* many), and who want to get on with something new and vital. Well, perhaps they'll find something to get their teeth into in this section. For the others, why not consider having a look at some of the less well-known aspects of colour work? I am an enthusiastic experimenter and you will find that you too will become more and more involved as your interest grows. But, as with everything else, don't try to run before you can walk. Master the basic principles first.

You should also acquire some knowledge of colour theory before proceeding to experimental work, as well as learning more about the materials you are going to use. So, let's start off with some tips on the sort of materials you are likely to want to use in colour experiments.

139

Materials for experiments in colour

Generally, the materials that you normally use are also used in colour experimentation. Personally, I work in 35mm format but I have made a point of equipping myself with a 6 × 6 cm enlarger so that I can work in the larger format if I need to. And it is sometimes necessary to work in a larger format for special effects, for example when re-copying a negative.

You will also need at various times Agfacolor positive M film (see tip 148), a soft sheet-film, for instance N-33p, and a hard sheet-film such as 081p. These are all Agfa-Gevaert products, available in 9 × 12 cm format, but there are many other sorts of black-and-white film on the market. You might also need an Agfa ME filter and a set of additive filters, texture screens (Paterson, for instance) Agfacontour film, black-and-white negatives, colour slides, and a contact printing frame.

Agfa positive M film

140 This is basically a sort of slide film produced in sheet form. It is designed for masked negatives and so an ME filter will be needed virtually always. With this film you can, for example, make colour negatives for slides or vice versa. You normally process it in dishes and you can use the ordinary 85 paper developing kit to do so. The times and concentrations are a little different than for paper, but there are no other problems.

You can use a No 13 (dark amber) safelight at least 1·5 m away, but you should not leave this material too long in any sort of light. You must also ensure intensive agitation in the dishes during processing. Overall, this is a very useful material, with a range of uses much wider than the few named above.

Copying

141 Many of the effects that are described in this section depend on copying for their effect. This is reverse copying, of course, in that a positive is made from a negative or vice versa. It is often done in a contact frame where the negative is simply laid on top of the sensitive material but it can also be done through the medium of the enlarger if it will work to a 1:1 magnification. If you make contact prints you can use the enlarger as your light source.

A good example of the sort of material normally used is the hard type of film such as Gevalith 081 or 081p (p = polyester), or soft types such as Gevalith N-33p. With the first sort you will get a negative or positive with very little half-tone, while with the second you will get all half-tone. Of course, these are both black-and-white materials, but they can still be used with colour negatives. For copying in colour you can use Agfa positive M film:

Processing positive M film

		Time (mins)	**Temp**
Paper developer*	85 CD	8	**(°C)**
Stopbath	5% acetic acid	3	20 ± 0,2
Washing		3	18-20
Bleach/fixer	85 BX	10	14-20
Washing		10	18-20
Final rinse	5 ml Agepon/litre + 15 ml formalin	1	14-20

* The 85 CD developer, in this process, is made up with a quantity one-third less than that recommended by the manufacturer so that the contents of a five-litre pack are in fact made up to 3.3 litres. This is because, at these concentrations, there is less likelihood of the oxidation that would occur in open dishes at the recommended concentrations.

142

Photograms in colour

I suppose you know what a photogram is? Well, it's a sort of photo made without the need for a negative, by simply laying an object directly on to photographic paper, putting it underneath a light source (usually the enlarger), and exposing for a predetermined period, after which the paper is developed. In our case we would have the light coming through a very dense filter (about 100 Durst or 200 Agfa). Thus we would obtain a photogram in colour. Using a 100 yellow filter you will get a blue photo with a white silhouette on it but you can also make photograms in two or three colours. For two colours, expose the paper with one colour as above, then remove the subject and expose with a second colour. If you want a third colour put the subject back, not necessarily in the same place, and expose again. There is an enormous range of possibilities; it is really only limited by your own imagination.

143

Variations on the photogram theme

It is always possible to put something else in place of the negative in the carrier of the enlarger. Something like, for example, buttons or soapsuds, bits of plastic, and so on. You won't be able to get these things in between the sheets of glass of the carrier but they will lie on top if you're careful. Now, using dense filters (100-200), you can make some really attractive patterns.

Again, you can use positive M film in place of paper. You then create a number of further ways of copying this positive film with or without filters, or perhaps making direct enlargements. As I say, the possibilities are endless – but so is the time taken so be patient, especially at the beginning.

144

Prints from slides

This is quite easily done but you have to remember to use an ME filter, because the slide has no masks and the paper is designed for films with masks. Of course, the print will come out in its complementary colours but this can be most effective. And you can put in or take out colour casts just as you wish by using filters. See tips 156-165.

Screens

145 Screens are used a great deal in black-and-white photography but not so much in colour. There are in essence two ways of making a pattern on your photograph. One is to use a special slide bearing the desired pattern sandwiched in the carrier with the negative. You can get these texture-screen negatives in various patterns from Paterson and they are available in 35 mm format or 6 × 6 cm. Alternatively you can make your own screens by photographing materials such as cloth, gauze, etc, and then turning them into positive screens by copying on to hard lith film. The other way is to use the materials themselves, enlarged along with the negative. You will find that if you use black-and-white slides as texture screens you will get a brownish colour cast in the print, but of course this can be removed by filtering.

Relief effects

146 Just as in black-and-white photography, this effect is created with a negative-positive sandwich. A positive transparency is overlaid on the negative, then slightly displaced. Clamped in this position in the carrier, a print is made of these two elements. You should use a good strong photograph for this but not one with a lot of fine detail. The positive copy should be quite soft, and this is best achieved by copying the negative on to black-and-white film. After development in ordinary black-and-white paper developer the effect can be checked by superimposing the two transparencies on a light box. Don't overdo it or you'll spoil things. You might also notice a few white spots shining through the dark parts of the positive.
You can, of course, do the copying on to positive M film. You will then obtain a very unusual slide, which you can either project as it is or print on to paper.

Pseudo-solarization

147 If you allow a rapid exposure to white light to occur during processing you get what is sometimes known as the Sabattier effect, but more commonly as pseudo-solarization. This is often done in black-and-white work but you can also do it with colour papers although the possibilities are rather fewer. What you do is to make an exposure in the normal way by filtering and doing all the usual things. Then develop the print for a couple of minutes after which you take it out of the dish of developer and put it in another dish filled with water. This is placed under the enlarger, the aperture of which must be set to f/16. You now switch on the light for about two seconds (with no negative in the carrier, of course), and then put the print back into the developer and complete the development. In some parts of the photo you will find that a magenta to red colouration has been brought in (see colour illustration E). You will have to decide whether you like this effect or not. The extra exposure does not have to be to white light and by using coloured light you can get some interesting effects.

148 **Pseudo-solarization using intermediate negatives**

There are more options open to you by using intermediate negatives and positives, although there is also a lot more work involved. You can use a whole range of materials, each with its own possibilities: black-and-white negatives, colour negatives, slides, whatever you want. The first step is to make a positive copy on to N33p, which will give you all the detail you need. This positive is then, as the second stage of the process, contacted on to M film under the enlarger using a dense filter such as a 200 yellow or an additive yellow filter. The new film is then given about five minutes' development in ordinary colour-paper developer after which it is removed, placed in a bath of water, and put under the enlarger. Once the water has settled down you give a quick exposure with or without a colour filter, although an ME or YM filter is generally used here. The film is then put back into the developer and processed as usual.

The negative you get in this way will be in two colours, although you can if you wish go on to repeat the process and get more.

149 **Faults in solarization**

As you will now be aware, solarization involves taking a print out of the developer at a particular point so as to re-expose it to white or coloured light. With positive M film this point lies about five minutes into the developing process. One great mistake that can be made with this technique, however, is to take the print out of the developer too soon. If there is not enough picture there the extra exposure will, as it were, overwhelm the emulsion and produce an overall very dense colouration which is not what you want. The other thing is that the extra exposure must be kept short. Too long an exposure is fatal. In this respect, it may be worth considering working in three phases because this usually ensures a more even finish. The time of the extra exposure plays an even more important part in the solarization of a paper print. You can even do this by an amber safelight with a little practice. Again, it is often a matter of trial and error before you get the best results.

150 **Some more advice on solarization**

It may have occurred to you that this process is rather time-consuming, as indeed it is – it could well be too much to finish in one evening. Again, you might find that, in some cases, the image in the intermediate photographs is looking a little the worse for wear, which is rather off-putting. You must therefore try to avoid dust as much as possible, because its image is transmitted through all the succeeding phases. Again, the dish you use for exposing the print should be black or dark grey in colour to prevent the possibility of other colours being reflected into the picture from the walls of a coloured or white dish. Save time by cutting down on washing times for intermediate negatives and using a hair dryer for drying them. Look out for other variations such as using a texture screen and solarizing this. Further information on this technique can be got from other more detailed books, such as "Creative photography", by Hans Götze and ? "Enlarging in colour", by Jan van Welzen, both published by Focus-Elsevier; and "Creative darkroom techniques", a Kodak publication.

151 **Ten exposures on a single print!**

The colour photograph labelled G reproduced earlier in this book is a good example of superimposition technique. The slide was first copied on to Agfa N81p material and this gave a stark white figure on a black backkground. Some test exposures were then made for the colour filters that were going to be used; green, blue, yellow, red and purple. To give a little more "body", extra exposures were increased by one quarter between the main exposures so as to emphasize the intermediate tints.

Finally, the printing frame was precisely located on the baseboard and fixed in place with marks to indicate the degree of movement required. The actual printing was a rather time-consuming process because the paper had to be covered with a light-tight lid after each exposure so that the marks could be seen and the frame moved by the desired amount. The light was also needed to readjust the filter for each new colour.

152 **Superimposing text**

In the previous tip I told you how I superimposed one image on top of another on the same print. Well, you can use the same technique to make your own Christmas cards, New Year cards, or whatever you want to send. Set up the text you want on a white card using any one of a number of methods available to you nowadays. Photograph this on black-and-white film and then copy the negative onto line or lith film until you have a negative with white letters on a black ground. Then, after you've made the colour print, put the lettering negative into the carrier and a predetermined colour filter into the drawer. Then make the second exposure, making sure that the lettering falls on a light part of the photograph. After developing and processing you will have a colour photo with lettering on it in a colour of your choice.

153 **Spare filters**

Those of you who use a colour head will normally find that the maximum density available is ample for most uses. However, in special-effect work, for example in solarization, very high densities are sometimes needed; values of up to 300 are not unusual. The Durst 601 colour head gives a maximum density of only 100 but the Durst 605 goes up to 195. However these enlargers are fitted with a filter drawer so it is easy to add extra filters as required. 195CC value is 130 in densitometric value.

154

Agfacontour film

Also known as equal density film, this is a film which makes a positive and negative at the same time so as to get the so-called line effect. It is the only film in which the solarization effect is built in. The added advantage that it offers is that it is perfectly possible to obtain similar pictures every time. With solarization this cannot be guaranteed.

This film is most often used in the professional field, not only because it is quite tricky to use but because it is also far from cheap. In a book this size I can do no more than tell you that it is a fantastic material, and leave you to find out more for yourselves. If you want to do this, try two Fountain Press publications, "Günter Spitzing's darkroom book" or "Enlarging in colour", by Jan van Welzen.

155

Special effects at the time you take the photo

You should be thinking about special effects at the time you take the photo. Certainly you can get some marvellous effects. Nowadays there are some brilliant trick lens attachments which fit in front of the camera lens and produce some spectacular effects on the film. The ones most often encountered are the prism effects which produce a circle of three, five, or sometimes six repeated images. Best results are obtained with light subjects against dark backgrounds; street lighting, neon signs, and so forth give especially good results. Then there are the starburst attachments, which give that sparkling effect so often used in films and on TV, or the linear prisms that separate the picture into a number of strips (see colour illustration J). You can rotate these attachments to get the most dramatic result. You should use these with as large an aperture as you can, otherwise you might lose part of the effect.

8. Developing and printing from colour transparencies

A method of printing directly from colour transparencies has long been the dream of the amateur photographer. Now, at last, it has come true. There are two quite different types of materials both of which produce excellent results and the choice is a personal one because there are pros and cons for each.

156

Prints from colour transparencies

I'm no prophet, but since it is now possible for anyone to make good prints from slides without any of the bother that is associated with the process in the minds of many could it mean the eventual demise of the colour negative? I do not know. What I do know is that what was recently a no-man's-land has now become quite friendly terrain and that results which could not be guaranteed even for the professional have come within the reach of the amateur.

Formerly you had to make an intermediate negative by contact printing or with a slide copier using negative film so as to get the image in its complementary colours for printing on to paper. The ways you had of doing this were such that the final quality of the negative could be influenced by too many factors, such as exposure time, type of lighting, etc. Since the advent of reversal paper, however, all that has changed.

157

Kodak Ektachrome 14 RC paper

This is Kodak's contribution to the modern range of resin-coated reversal papers available for making direct prints from colour transparencies. The gradation of the paper has recently been improved and, so far as hardness is concerned, the fiercer highlights have been toned down and the skin tones are not so yellow. What is more, sensitivity has been improved to the extent that long exposures are now a thing of the past. Unfortunately it is only available in one grade so it is not possible to correct a contrasty or very flat transparency except by making a neutral grey mask.

Kodak supply a special developer for 14RC paper – process R-14 – which comes in a one-litre size. Tetenal also produce a kit, called High-speed process UK II, but the cheapest, quickest and best is Photochrome R.

158

Basic filters for Ektachrome reversal paper

Since you are now working with reversal paper you have to start thinking in reverse. The longer you expose this paper the lighter it gets, and the shorter the exposure the darker the result. When you use it, you must always have a UV filter such as the Kodak No CP-2B in the drawer. For correcting colour balance, filters of any make can be used.

You need a basic filter set consisting of a UV filter as mentioned above, and a set of subtractive filters. For the usual sort of lamp, your basic correction will consist of the UV filter plus five magenta (Durst cc value). If you use a halogen lamp (colour head), then you will need five yellow and 15 magenta in addition to the UV filter. These are just general values – the actual filtering will vary from case to case, depending on the colour cast of the enlarger and any corrections desired to the transparency.

159

Working with Ektachrome reversal paper

To start with, select a slide that has been well exposed and that has a certain amount of neutral grey in it. This will then be what you might call your "standard slide". Put the basic filter pack into the enlarger, and make a series of text exposures. In formats from 18 × 24 cm (8 × 10 in) down to miniature, set the aperture to f/8 and use exposure times of 5, 10, 20 and 40 seconds. In the vast majority of cases the resulting print will have a canary-yellow cast. You will, most probably, need to increase the magenta and cyan filters by Durst values of 15 M and 20 C to correct it. You will, incidentally, find that changes to filter values or to exposure times are very different from those used in processing negative film. Increases of 5 or 10 make very little difference to the result: you will need at least 15 or 20. The same applies to exposure times: one or two seconds either way is hardly noticeable.

To make absolutely sure that you assess the colour balance of your print correctly, check the grey areas, and do so after it has dried out. Kodak papers, in particular, have a blue cast when wet.

One of the best ways of working out the required correction is to use a Print Viewing card (see tip 100), remembering of course to take a filter in the complementary colour to that of the cast. So, for example, if the photo is too yellow you must use a blue filter to correct it. This sounds a lot worse than it actually is in practice and the big advantage of working with reversal film and paper is that, once you've got a good print, you can go on and process the rest of your transparencies, knowing that in the vast majority of cases the filters won't have to be changed. You'll only need to reset your system on another pack of paper that will have a different base value. In general it is absolutely true to say that, making prints direct from transparencies using either Kodak 14 RC or Ciba-chrome (see tip 161), you are more likely to get good results than if you are using the negative process.

Colour cast	Required correction	Filters that can be removed	Filters that can be added
Yellow	Blue	Yellow	Magenta+cyan
Magenta	Green	Magenta	Yellow+cyan
Cyan	Red	Cyan	Magenta+yellow
Blue	Yellow	Magenta+cyan	Yellow
Green	Magenta	Yellow+cyan	Magenta
Red	Cyan	Yellow+magenta	Cyan

Processing

In the instruction leaflet that you get with Kodak and Photochrome R materials you will see that there are two developers used and that you have to make an exposure to white light in between them. The first one is an ordinary black-and-white developer and has to be used in absolute darkness. After this you use a stopbath and then expose to white light for the appropriate time. Some people do not give the exposure straight away, but wash the print first. The print is then exposed for a few seconds about 40 cm (16 in) from 100-watt light bulb. There is no danger of overexposure. When the print comes out of the colour developer it will look a little grubby and it can't really be judged until after it has been bleached, washed and dried. Also, when it is wet, it will look too blue.

Ektaprint R-14 chemicals

First developer	60 ml	31 ± 0.3°C	3 minutes
Stopbath	60 ml	31 ± 1.0°C	1½ minutes
First wash (repeat twice)	± 250 ml	31 ± 1.0°	2 minutes

Intermediate exposure: about 15 sec, some 40 cm away from a 60 W bulb, emulsion side of paper towards lamp.

Colour developer	60 ml	31 ± 1.0°C	3½ minutes
Second wash (repeated twice)	± 250 ml	31 ± 1.0°C	2 minutes
Bleach-fixer	60 ml	31 ± 1.0° C	3 minutes
Third wash (repeated twice)	± 250 ml	31 ± 1.0°C	3 minutes
Stabilizer	60 ml	31 ± 1.0°C	1 minute
Fourth wash (recommended)	± 250 ml	31 ± 1.0°C	½minutes

The Cibachrome-A print system

161 Ilford market the Cibachrome-A system made by Ciba in Switzerland. This is a system aimed at the amateur, and it gives results similar to Kodak 14 RC for prints made direct from transparencies. Processing, however, differs from the Kodak 14 RC material because Cibachrome uses a silver-dye bleach principle and this system does not require an intermediate exposure.

What this means, in simple terms, is that while RC14 produces the image by means of colour producing substances or "couplers" contained in the developer, the Cibachrome material has the colour already contained in the emulsion and unwanted colour is bleached out during the processing. The base material is a white plastic instead of paper and the finished print has a very high gloss.

The system consists of a three-bath system – developer, bleach, and fixer. Processing takes place in 10½ to 13½ minutes, and must take place in a drum because this material is more than usually prone to damage while wet. In any case, the bleach has a very nasty smell, so you'll probably be just as pleased.

Processing with Cibachrome-A

162 One advantage of Cibachrome-A for the amateur is that filtering is very simple. A basic filter value is stated on the pack for all the most commonly available makes of transparency film.

If you keep to this, it will serve for 80% or more of your transparencies. Filter densities are given in Kodak values; if you want to use this with other filter packs you will have to convert the values as appropriate (see tip 94). You will also need a UV filter. If you still need a colour correction, proceed in the same way as described in the tips for Kodak 14 RC. You will, incidentally, find that this material is very resistant to fading.

The one thing you must be very careful about is the chemicals, especially the bleach. In every kit there is a neutralizer which must be used when disposing of chemicals. The bleach is a very strong alkali and can do a great deal of environmental harm, and ruin your pipes if not neutralized before throwing away.

Temperature	24°C±1½°C (77°F±·05°F)	20°C±1½°C (68°F±·05°F)	28°C±1½°C (82°F±·05°F)
1. Developer	2 minutes	2½ minutes	1½ minutes
2. Bleach	4 minutes	4½ minutes	3½ minutes
3. Fixer	3 minutes	3½ minutes	2½ minutes
Washing	3 minutes	3 minutes	3 minutes
Total time	12 minutes	13½ minutes	10½ minutes

You will need 90 ml of fluid to process a 20 × 25 cm (8 × 10 in) enlargement in a drum. Don't be tempted to experiment with quantities; they need to be exact. To help with this, the kit contains three measuring beakers. The life of the made-up solutions is as follows:–

Developer	two to four weeks depending on whether or not the bottle is completely full.
Bleach	four months.
Fixer	six months.

Developer and fixer can be split into smaller quantities but not the bleach.

163 **Developing transparency films yourself**

Well, why not? If you want to be a do-it-yourself darkroom artist, why not have a go at everything?

Of course, not all types of reversal film are suitable for home processing – CT 18 and CT 21, for example, along with the Kodachrome films. However, Agfachrome Professional and Kodak Ektachrome can both be handled in the amateur darkroom although you do need special packs of chemicals. These are made by the two principal companies as well as by the suppliers of universal packs.

Doing your own slides is not just a fad – there are advantages such as getting results quickly, reducing risk of loss during rush periods and less risk of damage and fog. All of which, I would say, are good reasons for doing it yourself.

164 **What to use for processing reversal film**

For both Agfachrome Professional films, 50S daylight and 50L artificial light, you have to use Agfachrome process 41. From a one-litre pack of this you can process twelve 35 mm films, and the instruction leaflet is very clear and concise. Because the developer doesn't keep, you should have a set of films ready for processing (holiday time is the most likely). The other solutions keep for up to eight weeks and you can buy chemicals separately.

Kodak offer two processing packs for their Ektachrome range – the E-3 kit, which needs intermediate exposure, and the E-4 kit, which does not. These processes are being superseded by E-6, which also does not need any intermediate exposure.

165 **Kits from other manufacturers**

To deal with Tetenal first there is:–

a. the Tetenal UA kit for Agfachrome, which will give you three 36-shot miniature films from 500 ml;

b. the Tetenal UK-X kit, intended for all Kodak films except Kodachrome. It has the same capacity as Tetenal UA but requires an intermediate exposure.

Processing with these materials has to be done at 30°C (86°F), and takes 37 minutes, including the final rinse.

Unicolor, on the other hand, have just the Unichrome kit which can be used for *all* colour reversal films except Kodachrome. A half-litre pack of this will do three miniature-format films but you can do a single film, if desired, by using only 250 ml. The chemicals come in fluid form and keep well.

9. Finishing

Now a few notes to make sure that you give your photos the finish they deserve.

66 **Finishing**

This is an aspect of colour photography which is strangely neglected. Far too often I see colour prints or transparencies with speckles and spots – it's really just carelessness because you can retouch colour photographs, and it's not as difficult as you might think.

Obviously, the real answer is to work in your darkroom with absolute cleanliness so that spots and speckles don't arise. But you know as well as I do that nothing is perfect and, in addition, there are other things that can happen that cannot be foreseen. So there can be good reasons for retouching colour photos; the potential exists so you might as well use it.

67 **Retouching**

What you will need is some slide paint (Schminke or Marshall), glossy retouching paint in colours and various shades of black and grey, and a retouching knife. The slide paint I referred to is a water-soluble paint available in more than forty colours, the strength and darkness of which can be altered still further by mixing with neutral grey. It can take a lot of time to get exactly the right colour but the results are marvellous. These paints penetrate into the emulsion and are therefore virtually invisible. They are also suitable for resin-coated papers. There are greys you can use for filling in white spots on parts of the image that are not absolutely black. This works because, as you will find, grey spots of less than about $\frac{1}{2}$ mm are almost unnoticeable. If a light spot occurs on a dark green or blue area, then black is probably the best colour to use. This is a big subject and you'd do well to read something like "Retouching" by Hans Götze (Fountain Press) if you want to take it further. For larger areas than spots, acrylic paints can be used but you have to be something of an artist to mix and match them.

168 **Scraping**

When there is a dark spot on a light area of a photograph you have to scrape it off with a retouching knife. You will find that, as you scrape away, the dark patch will first of all go blue, then magenta, then eventually yellow as you go down through the layers of the colour paper, so you will realize, that this scraping process is a job that has to be done with the greatest of care. Once you've finished the scraping-off the colour you want has to be applied carefully over the bare patch, using a suitable retouching paint. This will remain visible until the photo is sprayed with retouching lacquer. At one time this was used to ensure the lightproofing of the paper but nowadays it is more often needed to make the retouching work invisible. It comes in spray-cans with a choice of gloss or matt finish.

169 **Protective lacquer**

As we've already noted, protective lacquers are nowadays rarely needed for prints because of the resin-coating on modern papers. However, films still need protecting and Tetenal film-lacquer is good here. It helps to protect your films against scratches and also makes them anti-static, so reducing the dust that collects on them all too readily. If a film is already scratched you can use Tetenal Repolisan to get rid of the marks. The film is soaked in an undiluted bath of this solution and carefully dried in a dust-free atmosphere, after which all but the worst of scratches will have disappeared. It can be used over and over again and, if anything should go wrong, there is a special Repolisan solvent that will take it off again.

170 **Curling**

One of the more unfortunate phenomena associated with drying of prints is their tendency to curl. The causes of this are difficult to trace and range from storage of the material to rapid drying at too high a temperature.

Afga type 4 paper is poor as far as curling is concerned but type 5 is somewhat better in this respect. For myself, I would say that the Kodak 74 RC paper is best; certainly, I don't get much curling with this paper in my Durst drier. Cibachrome-A prints, being plastic based, dry very flat but other makes will usually lose their curl if placed on a cold surface while still hot from the drier.

171 **Mounting**

You will, of course, want to have your best work mounted, perhaps for exhibitions or even for your living-room wall.

There are not many adhesives which will give good results because of the resin-coating on the reverse side of your photo. And, in particular, you should not try any of the methods involving heat unless you have a special low heat mounter. Otherwise you will damage the coating on the front of the picture. There are adhesives that will work but they are not all that easily obtainable. My own best results have been obtained with a double-sided adhesive tape. Mounting pads are also good and spray adhesives like the 3M Photo Mount are very efficient although expensive and rather messy.

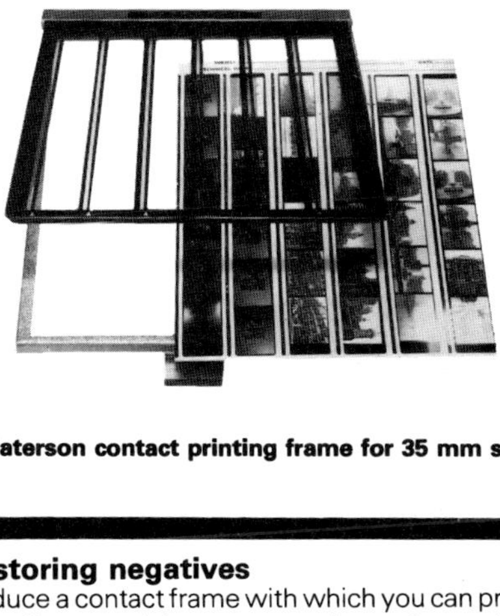

The Paterson contact printing frame for 35 mm strips

72 **Filing and storing negatives**

Paterson produce a contact frame with which you can print a whole film, either 6 × 6 cm or miniature on to a sheet of paper 20 × 25 cm (8 × 10 in). You can, of course, also use this for colour work. You cut up the film into six strips suitable for insertion into the frame and, when you've done so, make a small test strip without any filters (Y0/M0/C0). Determine the exposure in this way and then print the whole film on to a single sheet of paper using a basic correction filter (tip 87) if necessary. You can now take a good look over your whole film because you will have a sheet full of miniature prints. It is most likely that only the odd print will have the colour balance right, but you will at once be able to determine which ones have colour casts and what they are. When you have done that the sheet provides a perfect way of filing and storing your photographs. It can be stored, together with the strips of film, in the pages of a Paterson file or something similar. This will give you a complete filing system of indexed prints and negatives.

10. Special equipment and accessories

The task I've set myself here is really an impossible one, because there are new items coming out all the time and it would need a continuous article to keep up with them. So, if you find things I've missed – don't shoot the singer, he was only doing his best! Study the pages of the photographic magazines and you will always be up to date with new materials, chemicals and equipment.

The colour head

173 No doubt by now you will have seen a fair amount of text devoted to filters, filter-kits, drawers, and what-have-you. You will also have seen the term "colour head", and possibly wondered what it meant.

This is simply an apparatus on the enlarger which contains all the filters you need and they are controlled by turning a few knobs. It is a really useful thing to have in your darkroom and if I had to choose between this and other fancy bits of equipment like analysers, developing machines and so forth I would choose a colour head every time. The colour head has a number of advantages that will be outlined later. It is especially useful in combination with an analyser, although you can also use an analyser with separate filters in a filter drawer.

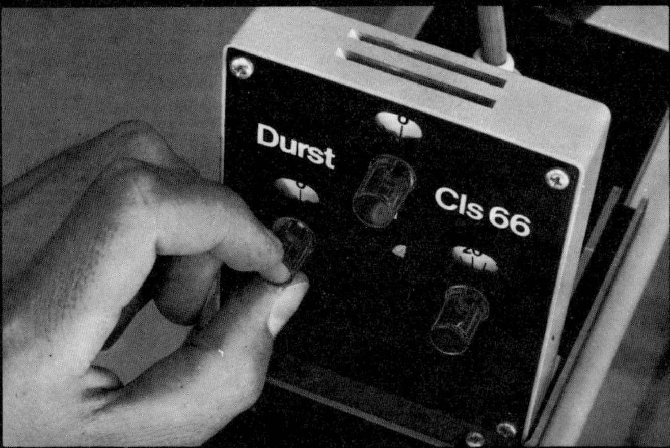

Advantages of the colour head

174 To a large extent the advantages speak for themselves. For a start, the head saves you time because it tells you exactly when a given filter is right. Then again, it works steplessly; that is to say you aren't limited to just the values in multiples of 5 or 10, but can get a magenta value, say, of 8. Thus it is also more accurate.

Colour heads usually employ a low-voltage halogen lamp, which doesn't change its colour temperature as it ages. Also, the lamp is normally a relatively "cold" light which, together with the reflected mirror arrangement, prevents overheating.

The condenser when fitted is used for black and white printing and is removed for colour work. For colour it is replaced by an opal glass which ensures an even light over the whole field, thus avoiding the speckles (and associated retouching) that can occur otherwise. Finally, the filters, partly because of the dichroic system, don't fade with use and being 'sharp-cut' they are more efficient because there is less overlapping.

The Meochrom colour head

175 The famous Czech firm that produces the Opemus 3/4 and Axomat 2/3 enlargers also has a colour head on the market. In view of the extent to which their enlargers are used in Europe it is not surprising that they have come out with this as well. Naturally, it fits all enlargers of these types – the Axomat 3 and Opemus 4 without adjustment – although older types will require an extra fitting for the filter drawer because of the distance between the colour head and the condenser. Durst Omega, Kaiser, Leitz, Krokus and Vivitar also make enlargers fitted with colour heads.

The meochrom instrument uses a complete set of subtractive filters of 7.5 cm square format, continuously variable from 1 to 150 in Agfa values. The light source is an ordinary 12V, 100W halogen lamp fitted into a reflector. Because this head does not require a special reflector bulb, it works out a little cheaper.

176 A Durst colour mixing head (left) which employs dichroic filters that can be 'dialled in' by turning three knobs – yellow, magenta and cyan. They are calibrated on the latest model up to Durst value 130 (Kodak cc 195) and the windows are illuminated for easy reading in the dark. The new 605 model also has a supplementary filter equivalent to 40 yellow + 40 magenta, which increases the filter density to 170 (Kodak cc 255) for these colours. Illumination is by a reflex system using a 12 volt 100 watt tungsten-halogen lamp which has a constant light output throughout its life.

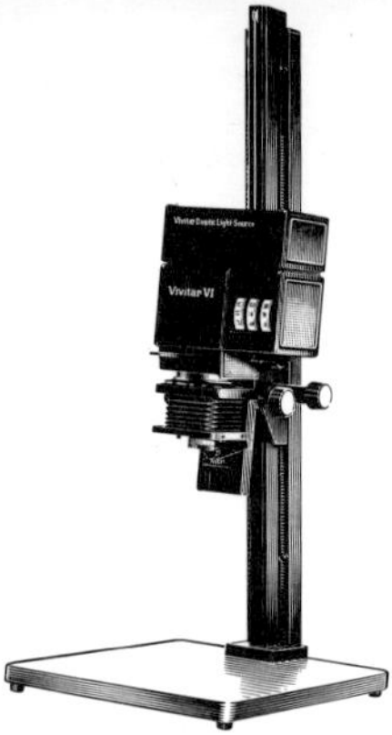

The Meochrom colour head

Compete colour enlargers

There are now complete colour enlargers designed specially with the amateur in mind available from several different firms. What I mean by a complete colour enlarger is one that is supplied complete with colour head, all ready for use although most of them also have a filter drawer.
Durst make the M 301, M 601 and M 605 especially for colour work. Kaiser, Rollei and Vivitar have also produced enlargers with built-in colour heads.
The Kaiser enlarger, like the Durst 605, goes up to maximum filter density of 195 Kodak but it is impossible to keep up to date because the great interest in colour printing is encouraging manufacturers to bring out new enlargers for this purpose. Again, the photo press will keep you up to date.

The Durst 301 enlarger with built-in colour head

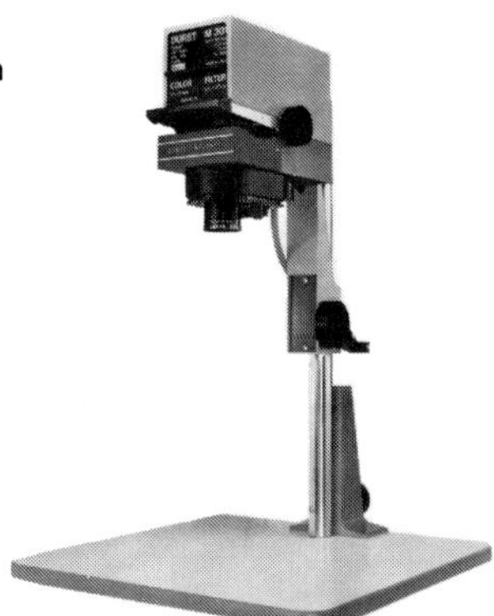

178 **Analysers**

These devices have been in use in black-and-white processing work, where they were used to determine exposure and grade of paper, for some years. Now they are available especially for colour printing, and they give you correct filtration.

Of course, you can work without an analyser. It will, however, save you an awful lot of time when it comes to determining what filters to use and what is more it will do this very accurately. Against this you must set the fact that, compared with other equipment that you will be using, the cost is considerable. Even apart from the sort of thing that only professionals can afford, you will have to pay £100 or more for one.

179 **The principle of the analyser**

All analysers intended for the amateur market work on the same principle. The integral measuring system, as it is called, which gives a total measurement of the three main colours. You start with an ''ideal negative'' which has been worked out manually to have neutral colour characteristics. This is used as a datum and then other negatives can be compared with it by using the analyser. Just what percentage of the negatives will give a good result depends on the sensitivity, the electronic components and the measurement method used but, with high-quality apparatus, you should get between 80% and 90%. Only negatives that have a really pronounced colour cast will be so far from the ideal negative that they cannot be dealt with.

180 In order to use an analyser you first need to make an ''ideal'' print from the neutral ''ideal'' negative. To do this all the filters should be moved out of the light path and a test print made to establish the correct exposure by using a Durst Comask, or masking in stages as you would for a black and white print. This is almost certain to show some colour cast which must be neutralised by a filter or combination of filters of the same colour. A further print or prints are then made until a perfect print is achieved and the filter factors, exposure and magnification carefully noted.

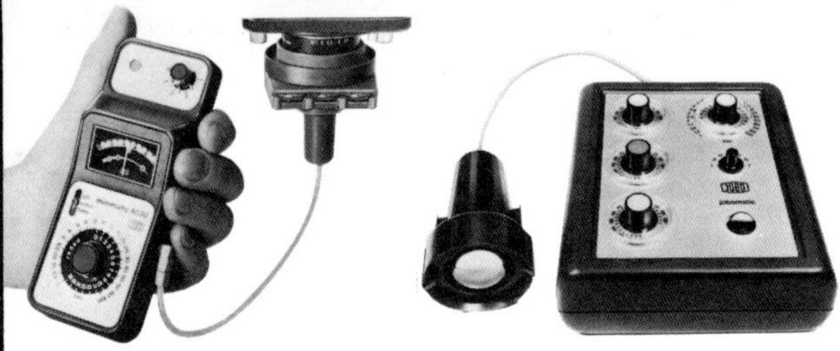

Left: the Jobo minimatic colour analyser
Right: the Jobomatic analyser

181 Always use only one or two – never three – filter colours. The stronger the colour cast, the higher the filter values must be. This increases the necessary exposure and the factors listed in the next tip can be used in this equation:–

$$\text{New time} = \text{Old time} \times \frac{\text{new filter factors } F1 \times F2 \times F3}{\text{old filter factors } F1 \times F2 \times F3}$$

There are also charts to do this for you and the Durst colour calculator makes it easy. The table below gives an abbreviated guide to exposure multiplication factors.

182

Kodak values	Yellow	Magenta	Cyan
05	1.02	1.08	1.06
10	1.04	1.15	1.11
20	1.08	1.26	1.20
30	1.11	1.36	1.28
40	1.13	1.44	1.34
50	1.15	1.52	1.40
70	1.18	1.68	1.52
100	1.20	1.92	1.64
130	1.22	2.16	1.76

The Philips PCA-060 colour analyser

183 This colour analyser from Philips, which determines the filtering requirement and the exposure time gives direct readings and is easy to use. It costs less than £100.

It has an integral measuring system by means of an optically intensified photo-diode cell which rests on the baseboard. There are motorized filters which select each colour channel in turn, and the light intensity in that range is measured by the photo-diode and transmitted to the analyser box. The filters in the probe are set up by fingertip controls located on the analyser box and the control knobs have a motion stiff enough to prevent them being knocked off setting. There are also numerals which allow you to make a note for future reference and which also allow separate settings to be made for different combinations. The knobs for the three colours are illuminated, as is the meter.

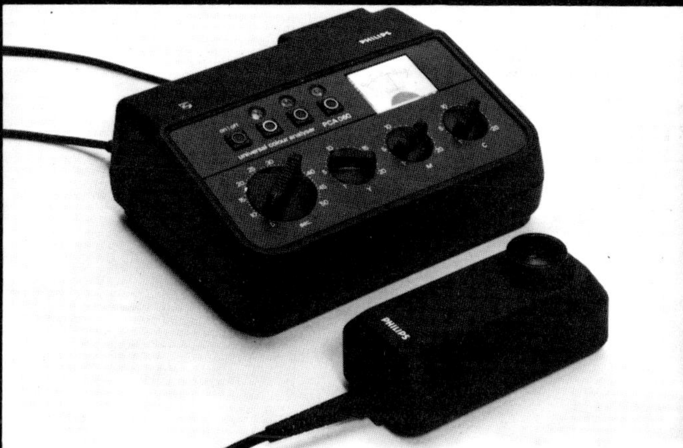

184 Setting-up the Philips PCA-060

This analyser also uses the principle of the ideal negative as a standard. Maximum light intensity is first determined by means of a removable diffuser. The cyan setting button is then pressed to bring the cyan filter into operation and the maximum reading on the meter is obtained by adjusting the cyan and exposure-time knobs. This then gives the base time obtained from the standard negative and similar times are obtained for the other two primary colours in the same way.

Determination of exposure time is done mainly through the cyan channel but can also be done through either of the other two. For those who don't have a filter head on their enlargers, there is a special holder on the probe to take 7 × 7 cm filters. This is easier than fiddling about with the filter drawer.

A large test-plate is enclosed with the analyser when you purchase it. By photographing this, you can make an ideal negative and also a test photograph.

Using the Philips PCA-060

185 Once set up, you proceed in the following way. First of all, remove the diffuser and make sure that you have no filters in between the enlarger and the probe. Press the cyan button and, by moving the probe and rotating the time knob, obtain the exact exposure time. Then, without moving the probe again or making any other alterations, press the magenta and yellow buttons respectively while setting up the filters in the colour head of the enlarger to get a zero reading on the meter each time. If you want to be really finicky, you can make a test print with the filter values and exposure time so obtained, but in my experience this is unnecessary.

You can also use this analyser for additive processing methods and for making prints direct from transparencies. The only small disadvantage I would comment on is that, for every variation in the base value the analyser has to be reset – using the unlit exposure knob!

The Durst Colorneg III

186 One of the most striking things about this Durst analyser is its very small size – not much bigger than a box of matches. The whole system, in fact, consists of two of these boxes, and is fitted with a three-position slide. The analyser is fastened under the lens with a clamp, and is powered by two PX 23 batteries. The Luxoneg, which is the lightmeter end of it, is just as small and is powered by one PX 23. It is an integral measuring device, working from an ideal negative. Setting up is done with a little screwdriver that screws inside the analyser and it cannot be moved accidentally. Once set up, there is little further need to regulate it.

The Luxoneg exposure meter which comes with the Colorneg analyser makes calculations of variations from format unnecessary so this is really a simple system. For my money, Durst have more than made up for the deficiencies of their first analyser with this Colorneg III

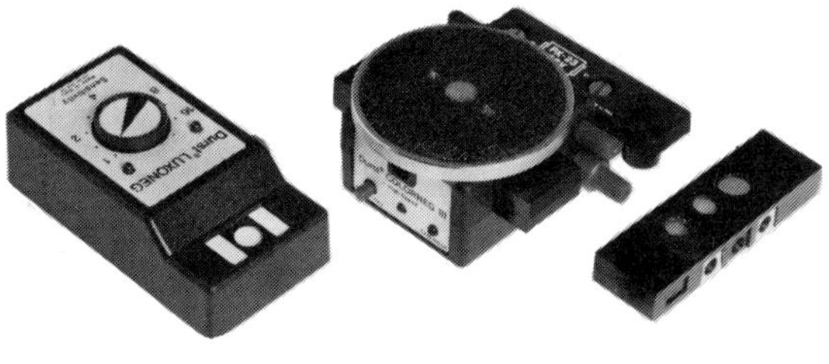

The Durst Colorneg III analyser is hardly any bigger than a box of matches.

Left: the Luxoneg lightmeter.

187 **Setting up the Colorneg III system**

The first thing to remember about setting up the analyser is that you have to wait about one minute after the enlarger is switched on so that the photocell reaches its maximum sensitivity.
The Luxoneg is set up by first of all swinging aside the analyser, and placing a special diffusing lens over the aperture. The safelight must be switched off as well to make sure that the only light reaching the measuring aperture is that from the enlarger. Then, by turning the knob on the device until the two lamps are balanced, the aperture to use is indicated.
This is one of those things that is a lot harder to describe than it is to do. So don't be put off. It's really quite simple and a detailed instruction book goes with it.

188 **Working with the Colorneg III**

A significant difference from most other analysers is that you begin with cyan, and move the filter ring to the left. The measuring head is set at zero for all filters, or there should be no filters in the drawer if a colour head is not used. The aperture is then altered with the red knob until both lamps are equally bright. You next go on to magenta, and turn the magenta knob from zero up to a value where both lamps are equally bright, and then go on to do the same thing for yellow. If you use loose filters from a filter pack you change the values of those in the drawer to get the same result. That is the process in a nutshell. As you might imagine, there is a lot more to it than that but space forbids going into it in more detail. With normal negatives you may have to make one or two proofs, although the number required could be higher with more difficult subjects.

189 **More expensive analysers**

The Omega analyser is extremely accurate and is capable of making spot measurements as well as overall averages. It costs over £100. As you might imagine, this instrument is more for the professional than the amateur. In any case, spot measurement isn't such an undisguised blessing as you might think. If it isn't used precisely it can lead to very much worse results than would have been obtained by normal integral diffusion methods.
There are other expensive analysers such as the Gossen Labocolor and the Jobomatic. Remembering the worldwide reputation of Gossen, I think that their analyser is a very interesting proposition but neither the Gossen nor the Jobomatic are readily available in the UK at the time of writing.

190

A warning about interchangeable lenses

There are probably quite a lot of amateurs who use a dual-format system, with a 75 mm lens for 6 × 6 cm and a 50 mm for 35 mm or less. It may well be that these lenses come from different manufacturers and can therefore differ in optical properties. What you may not realize, if this is the case so far as you are concerned, is that they may also have different colour characteristics. So if you set up your analyser with one lens in place and then change lenses you may well find that your colour balance is wrong. If you find that this is so, there is nothing else to do but reset every time you change lenses.

191

The ideal negative

When we were discussing the setting up of a colour analyser the term "ideal negative" was used and you may well wonder what this entails. Well, first of all, it must have been correctly exposed – over-exposed negs are definitely no good for this job. Also, there must be no dominant colour – no large areas of blue sky, great clumps of green trees, or anything like that.

Handbooks for analysers using the integral method usually refer to a street scene as being ideal. I would agree with, so long as it is stressed that a street scene does not mean monotonously coloured bricks and stones.

192

Making your own ideal negative

The sort of thing I'd advise you to look for is a market scene, in which a lot of different colours are present in the form of scattered small areas. If you want to go out and take a suitable photo, choose a sunny but slightly overcast day and see that you include in your shot some colourful fruit and flowers on market stalls, a bit of blue sky, a bit of grey awning, and a bit of road. Shoot the scene from different angles and make several different exposures. With this sort of shot and a little luck you should get an "ideal negative".

If you want to do a really good job I recommend you to make several negatives. The differences between papers and films of various makes are quite large enough to justify having a set of ideal negatives, one for each film/paper combination.

Agitators for developing drums

Drums used for developing paper must be agitated during processing. This can, of course, be done by rolling the tank back and forth manually but I can't recommend this as a regular process unless you want biceps like Charles Atlas!

For those who don't want to enter the Mr Universe competition there are various mechanical agitators on the market. Beseler, for instance, provide a simple electric motor roller, Unicolor have their Uniroller, Kindermann do the RC-N agitator with lateral as well as rotary motion and the Jobo CPE processor is motor driven.

All these devices provide rhythmic agitation for the drum and they can also be used for developing films. An extra refinement is provided by Jobo with the Colorprocessor CPE, which rotates in a water-jacket and can therefore be maintained at a constant temperature.

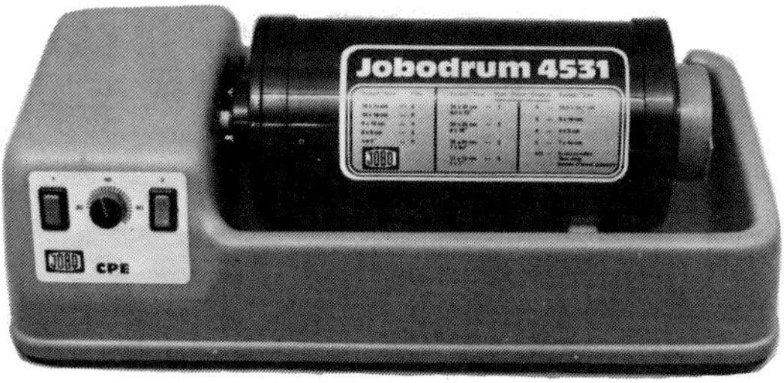

The Jobo CPE processor which drives the drum in a reciprocal action in a water bath.

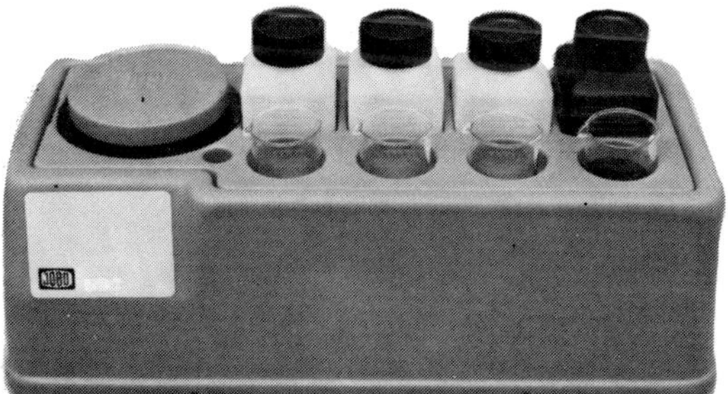

The Jobo TBE thermotank with a built in heater that maintains the solutions at a constant temperature.

The Jobo CPE Colorprocessor

The word for this equipment is, perhaps, "luxurious". In fact, I'd go as far as to say that, if you happen to see one demonstrated, you'll be sold.

This machine can be used for both Jobo paper developing drums as well as for the special film tanks.The drum is fitted with a ring magnet which rotates when inserted into the machine. The lateral agitation has two speeds – fast for paper and slow for films. The built-in heater can be thermostatically controlled with incredible accuracy – up to 0.2°C. The drum rotates in a water-bath and the water is constantly recirculated to ensure that the temperature is maintained within these limits. It will process all film sizes up to 9 × 12 cm (4 × 5 in) and paper up to 40 × 50 cm (16 × 20 in).

There are recesses for four one-litre bottles and smaller recesses to take measuring cylinders so that the fluids used can also be kept at the appropriate temperature. An even more luxurious model, called the CPP, has four adjustable temperature settings, four separate programme controllers, and four programme buttons. An automatic cooler can be provided so that you can rapidly come down to a lower temperature if need be.

As you can imagine, the processing time with this equipment is very fast. If, for example, you work with two drums you can keep the working chemicals warm in their measuring glasses and very quickly change over the drum for one which has been washed out and dried. In fact, it is possible to have a print finished within four minutes if you work with these machines at a high enough temperature. So, as you can see, they are quite something.

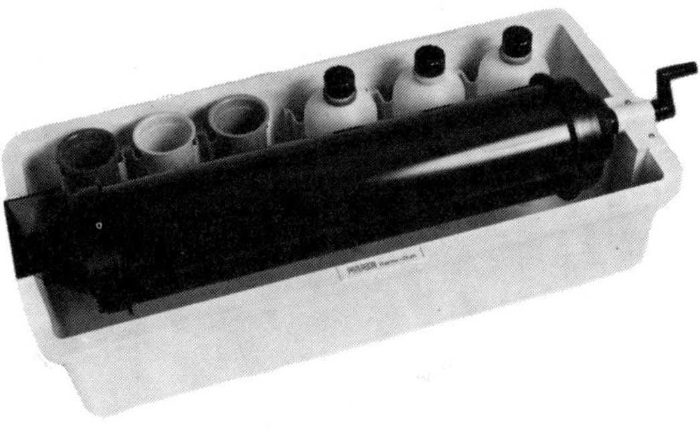

The Paterson tank for large prints. It is not heated but temperature is easily controlled.

195 **The Jobo 2400 daylight film tank**

In a period in which we seem to have almost everything for the darkroom, I still think that this new Jobo film tank is worth a tip. In my view, this is the simplest and the safest daylight film tank around. A 35 mm film cassette is very simply inserted into the tank and the end of the film is led onto the first teeth of the spiral. The tank is then closed and a simple system winds the film out of the cassette and clips it off at the end. The empty shell can then be removed from the tank. In this way, the film is loaded with complete safety and it is possible to develop smaller pieces of film in this way, too. It costs around £20.

196 **The Philips electronic timer**

I really would like to recommend to you this excellent electronic switched timer from Philips. Maximum time available is 99.9 sec, switching load is 500 watts, and the consumption of the timer itself is 10 watts.

The three knobs represent respectively tens, units, and tenths of seconds, so that, if the first knob is set at 2, the second at 4 and the third at 4, the time selected is 24.4 sec. A knob left at zero represents zero. When the clock is on, and the slide at the top left is in the left position, a red light comes on to show that the enlarger is switched on. Put the sliding switch to the right and both enlarger and red light go out while the time is held. You can use the knob at the right hand side to start by pressing it in. The time can be held indifinitely without altering the setting knobs.

Finally, as this timer is stabilized against variations in the mains voltage, it is extremely accurate and very useful in colour work. It costs about £28.

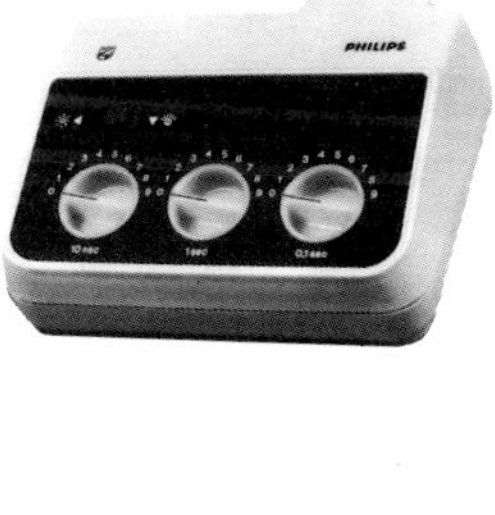

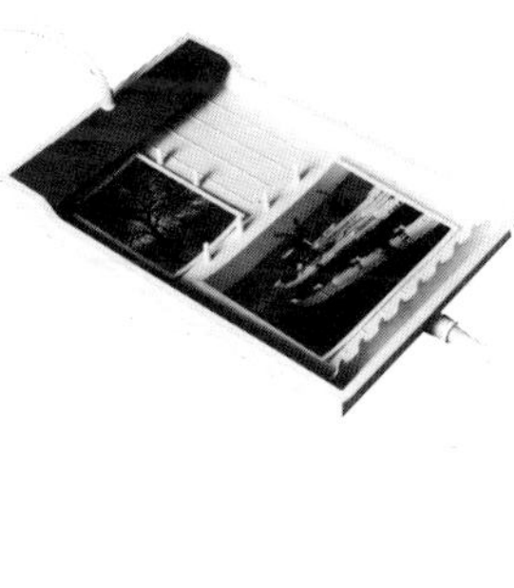

Left: Philips electronic timer

Right: Paterson high-speed print washing apparatus

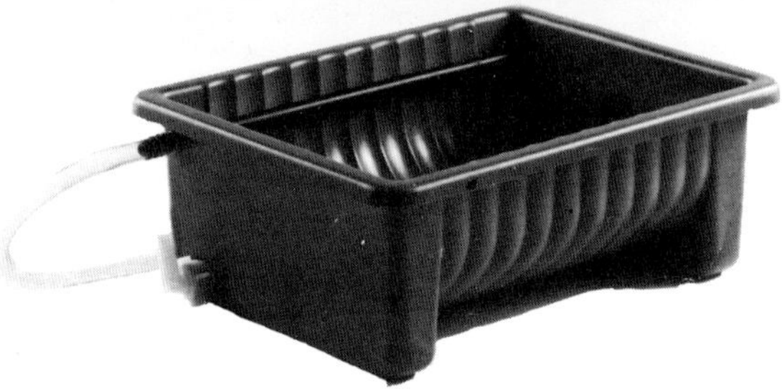

The Durst washing tank

197 Washing equipment for resin coated papers

Because of the short rinse-times recommended for resin-coated papers, there is some special equipment available. Durst, for example, produce a washing tank which ensures that the rinsing water is completely changed once a minute. In a three-minute wash period, therefore, you get three completely fresh lots of water over your print.
Jobo do a sort of flat trough in which the prints are individually held. Water can then be sluiced over them using the Jobo Cascade. There are two models, one of which will take four 18 × 24 cm prints and the other will wash two prints 18 × 24 cm.
Paterson also make a good print washer. As the photograph shows, it consists of a shallow trough which has ridges on the bottom, and also inlet and outlet hoses. Plastic pins can then be inserted in various formats, as required, and typical arrangements that can be processed at once are, for instance, one 30 × 40 cm print, two 20 × 25 cm prints (8 × 10 in) or four 13 × 18 cm (whole plate) prints.

198 Paterson water filters

In some places the water supply is not all it might be. This is not necessarily a fault of the locality because it can also be caused by old water pipes in a house. Whatever the cause, thick brown trickles are not much good in your darkroom and washing prints with water of this quality can be disastrous.
If this is a problem where you are the Paterson filter may be just what you need. It connects to the tap with a flexible hose and leads the water through a 20-micron stainless steel filter which removes all the potentially damaging particles. The filter is easy to clean and is replaceable. It's not too expensive, either.

199 **Drying equipment for resin-coated papers**

I think we can safely say, nowadays, that the age of the drying and glazing press is past. Resin-coated papers don't need it. In fact excessive heat can damage them! What they do need is a little help to dry out perfectly and that is provided by several useful devices, some of which are described below.

There are various choices from Durst. There is the small FCR-200, taking two 20 × 25 cm (8 × 10 in) prints, or the larger FCR-400, which will take up to five prints of 30 × 40 cm (12 × 15 in) or less. The latter is also provided with a sort of wringer through which most of the water is squeezed out of the print and can then be very rapidly dried in filtered warm air in about five minutes. The rubber rollers of the wringer must be carefully dried after use, otherwise they can stick together. Durst also do the UT-100 for drying films. This is a dryer that can be hung up and has a fan and filter. It comes in two sizes – one with a short plastic drying bag for use with prints and the other longer model for films. Both these models are provided with zip fasteners and can be folded into a small space when not in use.

Kaiser do two models for prints which are rather similar to the Durst FCR range, and have wringers with rubber rollers. The 4021 will take three 18 × 24 cm (8 × 10 in) prints, and the 4022 four 30 × 40 cm (12 × 15 in). The photos are held one above the other in a sort of drawer and take three to four minutes to dry.

200 **Variations in mains voltage**

Your enlarger lamp has a particular colour temperature. If by any chance the mains voltage drops the lamp will burn less brightly and it will also give off light of a lower colour temperature. This is of little importance in black-and-white work but in colour it can make a big difference to your results. It can make you choose filters too much on the green side because the lamp is too red. If your area is prone to this sort of trouble at peak periods I would advise you to consider investing in a voltage regulator. There is one made by Philips but it is rather expensive. If you use a colour head, you will have a low voltage halogen lamp and voltage variations with these are minimal.

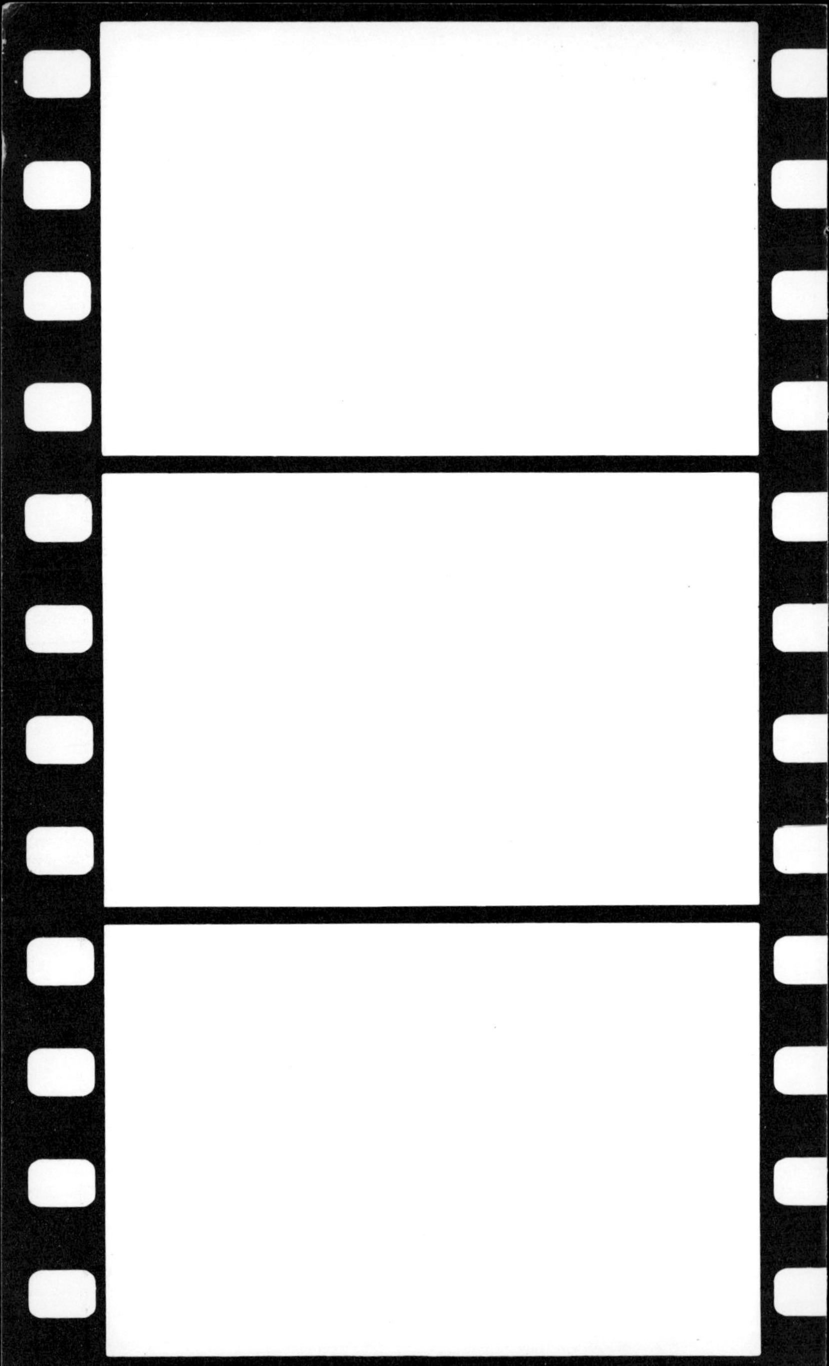

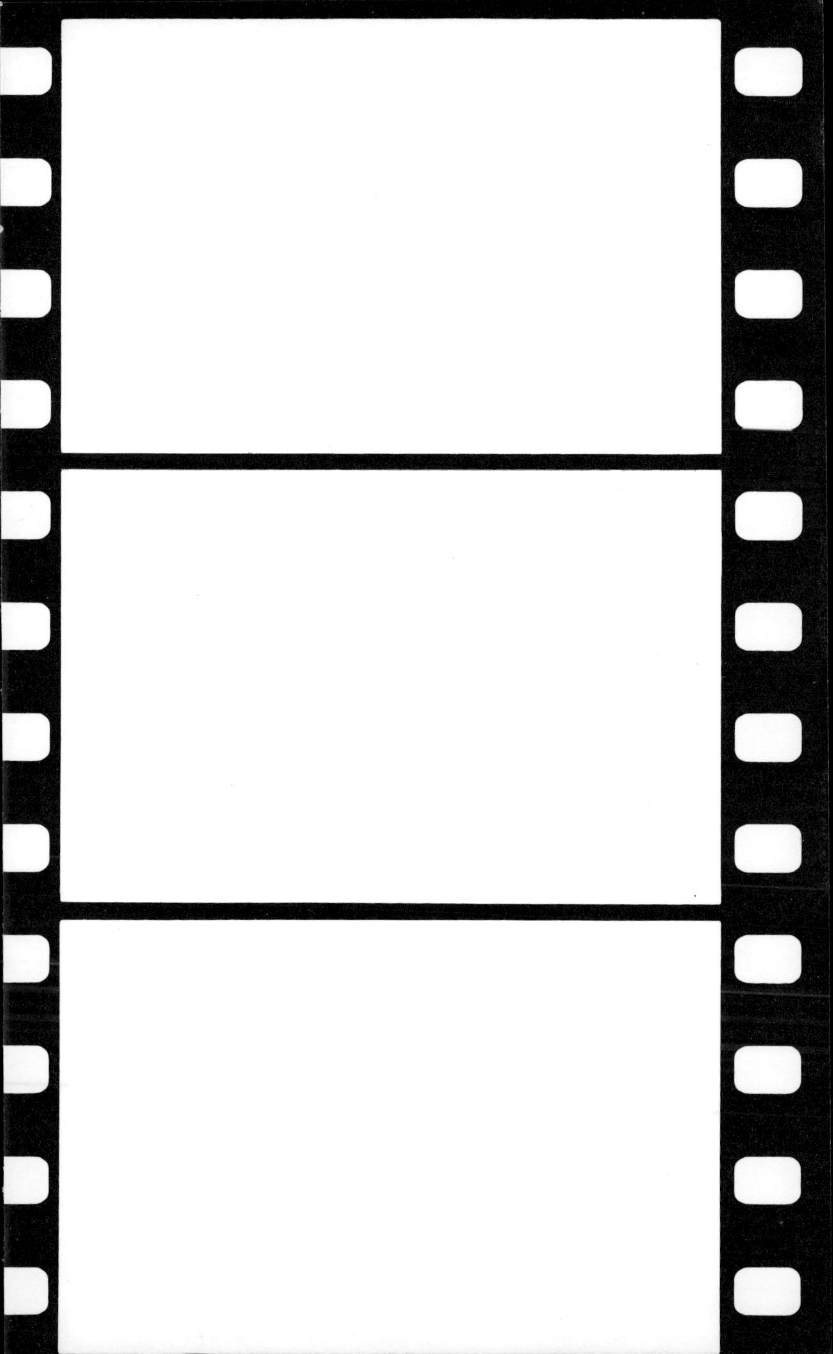

Other titles in this series:

E. Voogel and P. Keyzer

200 ciné tips
200 slide tips
200 flashtips
200 darkroom tips – black and white

Gunter Spitzing

200 filter and lens tips
200 phototips